CONFLICT IN
INTIMATE RELATIONSHIPS

THE GUILFORD SERIES
ON PERSONAL RELATIONSHIPS

Steve Duck, Editor
Department of Communication Studies
University of Iowa

CONFLICT IN INTIMATE RELATIONSHIPS
Dudley D. Cahn

FRIENDSHIPS BETWEEN WOMEN: A CRITICAL REVIEW
Pat O'Connor

CONFLICT IN INTIMATE RELATIONSHIPS

by
Dudley D. Cahn

THE GUILFORD PRESS
New York / London

© **The Guilford Press 1992**
A Division of Guilford Publications, Inc.
72 Spring Street, New York, N. Y. 10012

Printed in the United States of America

This book is printed on acid-free paper.

Last digit is print number: 9 8 7 6 5 4 3 2 1

Library of Congress Cataloging-in-Publication Data

Cahn, Dudley D.
  Conflict in intimate relationships   /   by Dudley D. Cahn
    p.   cm. — (Guilford series on personal relationships)
  Includes bibliographical references and index.
  ISBN 0-89862-975-6 (hard). — ISBN 0-89862-982-9 (paper)
  1. Marital psychotherapy. 2. Interpersonal conflict. 3. Di-
vorce mediation. 4. Intimacy.   I. Title. II. Series.
  [DNLM: 1. Conflict (psychology). 2. Interpersonal rela-
tions. BF 683 C132c]
RC488.5.C325 1992
158'.24—dc20
DNLM/DLC
for Library of Congress   92-1556
                                                              CIP

To Jeffrey and Leanne Richards
  as a wedding gift
and to Helen and William Gielincki
  in honor of their 50th wedding anniversary

PREFACE

The more one studies interpersonal communication, especially in intimate relationships, the more one sees conflict or opportunities for conflict. Outright arguments and disagreements may occur, but many other types of interaction also may involve conflict. For example, simply putting a question to one's partner may produce an unexpected response that makes one regret asking. Or, when one answers a partner's question, feedback from the questioner may indicate displeasure, surprise, anger, or other negative reaction. If one really wants to take a risk, one may try to give advice to a partner. Every time partners indicate their interests, points of view, or opinions, they run the risk of conflict. While these conflicts may appear minor, they have potential for serious negative consequences.

As pervasive as conflict is, the threat of conflict need not discourage partners from interacting. It does, however, call attention to the need for dealing with conflict and keeping it within bounds.

Early works on the subject, such as that of Bach and Wyden (1968), were more practical than theoretical: designed to provide intimates with techniques for "fighting fair in love and marriage." The present book, by contrast, is intended to bridge the gap between theory and practice on this important subject in a way that is more useful to social science researchers and students. It is applicable to the expanding field of work on personal relationships that now encompasses social, clinical, and developmental psychology, communication studies, and marital–family studies.

The first problem one encounters when attempting to pull together theory and practice is the extensive nature of the empirical research on intimates in conflict. Numerous empirical studies appear in several related disciplines, such as psychology, communication, and family studies. Moreover, a review of the literature can be confusing because the studies appear to reflect different orientations to research, use different types of measures, and have their own jargon. The first step then is to identify the major perspectives on gathering data and to organize the theory-driven studies along the lines of these research approaches.

A second problem is that more than one perspective or approach appear to dominate research on intimates in conflict. Another important step then is to describe, compare, and contrast these major approaches.

The audience for this book is twofold. First, the book is written for upper-level undergraduates and graduate students who are interested in the subject of interpersonal conflict applied specifically to intimate relationships. While many books cover marital communication or intimate relationships, they usually fail to deal directly with the topic of *conflict*. Also, the few available books that deal with interpersonal conflict are much more general in nature. The book is additionally intended as outside reading for advanced courses in related subjects such as interpersonal communication, male–female communication, marital communication, and personal relationships, where conflict may appear as a unit of study.

Second, the book is also written for researchers who are studying conflict between intimates. The book confronts many fundamental issues and questions regarding theory and research, and surveys a range of studies in which critiques of the areas have been missing. Before researchers on conflict and intimacy expend a great deal of time and energy gathering data, they should ask themselves what they are trying to do, what measures are most appropriate, how to define conflict, and what assumptions they are making about the conflict and intimacy processes. By comparing and contrasting three approaches to the study of conflict and intimacy, this book offers perspective and clarifies research issues especially with regard to theory development and methodology. This book, therefore, is written from the viewpoint of the scholar–researcher and is designed to cross disciplines within the social sciences.

Conflict in Intimate Relationships is intended foremost to advance the study of conflict in intimate relationships. It is one of the few books that provides an overview and evaluation of theory-driven research on the subject.

Acknowledgments

Thanks to the award of a sabbatical leave, I was given the necessary time and freedom from teaching and administrative duties in the Department of Communication at the State University of New York, College at New Paltz, to greatly expand my review of the conflict literature and write this book. I would also like to express my appreciation to the faculty and staff at the Henry A. Murray Research Center, Radcliffe College, Cambridge, Massachusetts, for their sponsorship and conduct of the workshop Videotaped Couples Interaction Research, where I met many scholars of psychology, communication, and family studies, who are actively engaged in the study of conflict in intimate relationships. In particular, I would like to thank Drs. Howard Markman, Cliff Notarius, Bob Weiss, and Mary Anne Fitzpatrick who helped me better understand the use of behavioral coding schemes. I express my thanks to Drs. Jess Alberts, Robert A. Bell, Nancy A. Burrell, and Adelaide Haas, my wife, Sharon Cahn, the editorial staff at Guilford Press, and the anonymous reviewers for their comments on earlier versions of this manuscript. I acknowledge the assistance of Monica Agosta in the typing of the bibliography.

I would especially like to call attention to the support as well as time and effort given this project by Steve Duck, the series editor. Thanks to his many insightful comments and suggestions, I learned a lot from writing this book.

—D.D.C.

CONTENTS

ONE. Introduction: An Overview of Theory and   1
    Research on Conflict in Intimate
    Relationships
What Is Conflict Between Intimates?   2
Understanding Theory and Research   4
Three Research Paradigms   5

TWO. The Systems–Interactionist Perspective on   9
    Couple's Conflict Communication
Background   10
Conflict Communication and Relationship Satisfaction:
    Supporting Research within a Systems-Interactionist
    Approach   15
Conflict Training: Helping Couples Resolve Issues and
    Improve Their Intimate Relationship   32
Conclusion   36
Note   38

THREE. The Rules–Interventionist Perspective on   40
    Divorce Mediation
Background   42
Divorce Mediation: Supporting Research Within a
    Rules–Interventionist Approach   53
Structured Mediation: Helping Divorcing Spouses
    Settle Disputes   65
Conclusion   70

FOUR. The Cognitive–Exchange Perspective on   72
        Conflict in Developing Intimate
        Relationships
        Background   73
        *Conflict and Relationship Development: Supporting
           Research within a Cognitive–Exchange
           Approach*   82
        *Educating Intimate Partners about How to Manage
           Conflicts*   107
        Conclusion   112

FIVE. Epilogue   118

References   125

Author Index   143

Subject Index   147

ONE

INTRODUCTION: AN OVERVIEW OF THEORY AND RESEARCH ON CONFLICT IN INTIMATE RELATIONSHIPS

As much as intimates might like to avoid conflict, they are more likely than are acquaintances to engage in frequent and intense disagreements. Unfortunately, intimates typically react to their differences by planning and engaging in negative behavior that becomes increasingly destructive. Because conflict often brings out the worst in people, partners who find it difficult to deal effectively with their differences tend to be more unhappy and dissatisfied than partners who are better equipped for dealing with them (Fitzpatrick & Winke, 1979; Rands, Levinger, & Mellinger, 1981; Ting-Toomey, 1983a).

According to Gottman (1991), certain ways of dealing with conflict harm intimacy. First, the more excited and heated the conflict (in terms of physiological arousal, especially for men), the more likely intimate partners were to disengage from their relationship and break up over the next 3 years. Second, some patterns of conflict were more beneficial to the relationship in the long run even if they appeared less desirable at the time. Third, certain nonverbal behaviors during conflict (e.g., woman's disgust, man's miserable smile) predicted breakups later. The fact that certain communication behaviors and ways of dealing with conflict are associated with dissatisfaction and breakdowns in intimacy suggests that it is possible to better understand conflict and to help intimates deal with it more effectively.

1

WHAT IS CONFLICT BETWEEN INTIMATES?

According to Braiker and Kelley (1979), intimacy is a close personal relationship in which two persons are mutually dependent and engaged in joint actions. While many might comfortably label "intimate" a stable or a developing romantic relationship, questions arise about other cases. What about stormy marriages or on-again, off-again romantic relationships? What about marriages where spouses no longer feel romantic? What about spouses who are legally separated?

The position taken in this book is that couples are identified as intimate when they meet these three criteria: (1) they have experienced a close personal relationship in the recent past or at present, (2) they are mutually dependent, and (3) they are engaged in joint actions. Therefore, like romantic partners in a developing relationship, dissatisfied spouses who seek marital counseling and spouses engaged in divorce mediation may be viewed as intimate partners, even when they are temporarily or permanently separated, because of their close personal relationship in the immediate past. Regardless of the present emotional states or physical proximity of the partners, the closeness of their relationship has been and remains a factor; moreover, the partners are mutually dependent and engaged in joint actions. Because they meet the above three criteria, romantic partners in developing relationships, dissatisfied spouses engaged in marital problem solving, and separated spouses undergoing divorce mediation may be considered intimate partners.

What is meant by conflict between intimates? Essentially a conflict occurs when there is a disagreement, difference, or incompatibility. Taking a communication perspective of conflict, I (Cahn, 1990) identified three different types of communication that accounted for a great deal of research on conflict in intimate relationships.

Specific disagreements. Some researchers focus on a specific communication act or interaction, namely, an argument over a particular issue. Sometimes this disagreement is referred to as a difference of opinion or view, a complaint, criticism, hostile/coercive response, defensive behavior, or unpleasant action. In any case, a couple overtly disagrees on some issue.

Problem-solving discussion. Other researchers focus on a more encompassing communication situation known as a negotiation or bargaining session or problem-solving discussion, which may deal with an on-going problem consisting of more than one conflicting issue.

Unhappy/dissolving relationships. Finally, still other researchers study the general pattern of communication characteristic of dysfunctioning couples, stormy marriages, and couples who report that they are unhappy, dissatisfied, maladjusted, or seeking counseling. (p. 5)

Margolin and her colleagues have classified different types of conflict according to the "tactics" employed by the intimate partners. Margolin, Burman, and John (1989) claim that the Conflict Tactics Scale—Form N (CTS-N) (Straus, 1979) may be used to identify physically aggressive (PA), verbally aggressive (VA), withdrawing (WI) and nondistressed/low conflictive (ND) couples. Self-reported verbal aggression is likely to precede self-reported physical aggression (Stets, 1990).

In the context of intimacy, moreover, conflict is more than a disagreement, incompatibility between partners, or partner opposition; it is an enduring or persistent element of interaction. Since it endures, it can also change and develop in form over time. Thus, conflict is best viewed as a process.

Coombs (1987) and Coombs and Avrunin (1988) propose that conflict progresses through three specific stages.

Stage 1. Potential conflict is experienced within a partner when faced with a choice between two or more incompatible options or goals.

Stage 2. The conflict becomes an actuality when interaction reveals that the partners want different things, but they think that these differences can be resolved.

Stage 3. The conflict threatens the relationship when the

partners perceive that there is no mutually acceptable outcome and unwanted sacrifices must be made for resolving their differences. At the third stage, self-interests usually replace mutual interests, there are winners and losers, and exercises of power likely dominate the process. For some, this stage of the conflict process may bring an end to intimacy.

By viewing conflict as a process, Coombs observes that self-interest drives partners from stage 2 to stage 3, whereas common interest drives a couple from stage 3 to stage 2 or 1.

The realization that conflict is a process that plays an important role in intimate relationships leads one to the social scientific literature on the topic.

UNDERSTANDING THEORY AND RESEARCH

Scholars have learned that making a dominant paradigm explicit is one way to make sense out of the theory and research on a given topic. While a theory is "a set of inter-related propositions that suggest why events occur in the manner that they do" (Hoover, 1984, p. 38), a research paradigm consists of a set of assumptions shared by many theories (Infante, Rancer, & Womack, 1990). In this book, paradigm is used interchangeably with perspective or approach.

Conflict between intimates can usefully be explored from at least three research paradigms. These perspectives may be labeled the systems–interactionist, rules–interventionist, and cognitive–exchange approaches. The following chapters discuss these dominant research perspectives and their associated theories and research on conflict between intimates. For each approach, a particular relationship situation has emerged as typical and is known as the "paradigm case" (or commonly used experiment). Other empirical studies dealing with that particular relationship situation are not included in this book because they do not relate specifically to one of the dominant perspectives. Merely introduced below, each of these perspectives receives detailed treatment in later chapters.

THREE RESEARCH PARADIGMS

Chapter 2 presents the systems–interactionist approach to the study of conflict between intimates in satisfying and dissatisfying relationships. Researchers who operate within this approach (e.g., Watzlawick, Beavin, & Jackson, 1967) generally focus their attention on a couple's-problem solving interaction as the paradigm case or typical experimental situation. Conflict from this perspective may be viewed as emotional expressions of opposing views in which partners employ particular communication patterns. This approach to conflict emphasizes escalation of negative conflict communication behavior and its harm to intimacy.

Researchers who work within the systems–interactionist paradigm have invested considerable time and effort attempting to determine how couples can solve their problems without doing (more) harm to their intimate relationship. Concerned with the communication patterns that conflicting partners use, systems–interactionist research usually audiotapes or videotapes satisfied and dissatisfied couples engaged in problem solving for subsequent coding by trained raters. This paradigm appears to be most useful for identifying couples' conflict communication patterns that encourage or discourage intimacy.

In Chapter 3, the rules–interventionist approach is discussed and used to explain the divorce dispute resolution or mediation process. This approach sees conflict as rule governed, competitive in nature, and emotionally charged. Researchers who take a rules–interventionist approach to the study of mediation (e.g., Burrell, Donohue, & Allen, 1990; Donohue, Allen, & Burrell, 1988; Donohue, Burrell, & Allen, 1989) call attention to the role of a third party who helps divorcing partners end one relationship and begin another and who represents interests above his or her own (i.e., the couple's children's, society's) as the paradigm case involving intimate partners. The mediator attempts to resolve disputes by introducing into the conflict process rules and social interests that are not usually involved when conflict is limited to the couple itself. Compared to private conflicts that tend to occur in the privacy of one's own home or that involve only the partners themselves, conflict of this type is seen more as a social, public, and cultural event in that a mediator intervenes to help a divorcing couple reestablish and maintain communication. Moreover, specific mediator communication behaviors guide the mediation process toward agreements that are reasonable and mutually supportive.

The rules–interventionist approach to divorce mediation has generated studies designed to answer the question: What role does the mediator play in helping divorcing couples restore communication for the resolution of issues? This paradigm is useful for incorporating the actions of an impartial third party or mediator along with those of the divorcing couple in a triadic model to determine the effects of the mediator and the divorcing spouses on the outcome of the mediation process.

In Chapter 4, the cognitive–exchange approach to the study of conflict and intimate relationship development is discussed. Researchers within the cognitive–exchange approach distinguish between perceived rewards and costs (e.g., Blau, 1964; Emerson, 1976, 1981; Heider, 1958, Homans, 1961; Kelley, 1971) and other cognitive phenomena, especially as they influence a developing relationship (including romantic partners, friends, and roommates). Cognitive–exchange theories and research are especially useful for explaining the role of conflict in developing long-term intimate relationships that are taken as the paradigm case. Cognitive–exchange researchers view conflict as cognitive constructs, namely, strategies involving perceptions and intentions that range from direct confrontation to avoidance and in turn influence relationship commitment. Research conducted within this paradigm typically asks the relationship partners to fill out subjective measures known as self-reports in the form of questionnaires (i.e., paper-and-pencil tests).

Research from this perspective examines the role played by partners' cognitions (i.e., self–other perceptions and conflict management strategies) in relationship development or commitment. Questions of interest are among the following: What antecedent conditions influence one's choice of conflict management strategy? What alternative strategies are best for dealing with different sources of conflict?

The attempt to describe these three dominant research perspectives should be accompanied by two caveats. First, the paradigm case for each research approach suggests that each viewpoint has become the "preferred" basis for formulating clinical/educational practice with respect to a certain type of relationship such as dissatisfied partners or divorcing spouses. A "winner by acclamation" approach should be taken cautiously, however. The concentration on one type of relationship by each perspective can be explained otherwise. Possibilities include the length of time the topic of conflict is under programmatic study, the relatively limited number of different scholars who are engaged in such research, and the difficulty of obtaining data. In time, researchers may expand the range of paradigm cases to include more than the one type of intimate relationship that is presently most popular for each perspective.

Second, while an identification of the systems–interactionist, rules–interventionist, and cognitive–exchange research perspectives may be made, some researchers use different paradigms at different times. They sometimes collect self-report data for cause–effect analysis of cognition, but at other times they code behavioral data for interactional analysis. When a third person intervenes to help settle disputes in some interactions, researchers again switch paradigms. To better understand the theoretical contributions of research on intimates in conflict, it is necessary to extract from a study the methods and findings appropriate to one perspective or another. Although there are researchers who clearly identify with one and only one approach, a false impression may be given that other researchers "belong" to one camp or another when in fact they may have conducted different studies using different research perspectives. Without intending to label specific researchers as one type or another, this book attempts to keep separate the different contributions their research makes to each perspective.

Presently, conflict scholars are working at a time when more than one paradigm is available. The implication is that each paradigm asks different questions, looks at intimates in conflict in different ways, provides different methods of analysis, and formulates different explanations. As pointed out in Chapter 5, this book argues that a better understanding of conflict between intimates is achieved by advancing theory and research related to a particular research paradigm.

In addition, the three research perspectives have contributed to many theory-oriented studies that characterize relationship changes that are becoming increasingly typical in the lives of many American couples.

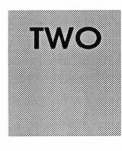# TWO

THE SYSTEMS–INTERACTIONIST PERSPECTIVE ON COUPLES' CONFLICT COMMUNICATION

Conflicts exist in varying degrees and complexity for intimates. As a conflict increases in degree and complexity, however, it goes beyond differences regarding a specific problem, issue, or argument because of the emotional nature of intimacy. In its most negative form, conflict is an emotionally charged event pattern that typically involves anger and hostility. Hostility might be expressed verbally as insults, name calling, sarcasm, and defamation which might result in partners' actions such as going home to mother at least temporarily, staying out all night, going to bars, physical aggressiveness and violence, or going out on a spending spree that a couple cannot afford, as well as inactions such as not speaking to each other, not answering the telephone, or not having sexual contact for a few nights or weeks. Thus, conflict between partners threatens their intimacy.

The conflict process may be defined as interaction between persons expressing opposing interests, views, or opinions (Bell & Blakeney, 1977). An approach to the study of conflict as a process that focuses on a couple's interaction patterns is the systems–interactionist paradigm (sometimes called the pragmatic paradigm), chosen by many theorists and researchers. According to this approach a couple's conflict communication is categorized as positive or negative according to its effects on the intimate nature of the couple's relationship. Usually, researchers who illustrate this approach to the study of conflict in intimate relationships recruit married couples as the paradigm case, create a conflict situation, and compare the conflict communication patterns of those who are satisfied with their marital relationship with those who are not. This chapter explores the basic approach and concludes with an evaluation of it as a research paradigm.

BACKGROUND

As is shown in the following sections, the systems–interactionist perspective has been influenced by social learning, cybernetics, information, and general systems theories.

Social Learning Theory

Like behaviorists generally, social learning researchers argue that most significant behavior is learned, subject to contingent reinforcement. When confronted with a novel situation, presumably organisms engage in random behavior. However, if favorable consequences result, the behavior is reinforced. In the future, a similar stimulus therefore leads to repetition of the reinforced behavior. If no consequences result, the behavior is not reinforced and therefore abandoned. When unfavorable consequences result, the tendency to avoid the punished behavior is reinforced. Reinforcement is called "conditioning" since the organism learns the conditions that are associated with each type of behavior and the response that it leads to. The tendency for an organism to respond similarly to a different but somewhat similar stimulus to which it was specifically conditioned is called stimulus generalization (Skinner, 1938).

In addition to focusing on behaviors and their consequences, systems–interactionist researchers learned from social learning theory the importance of quantifying and objectively measuring behaviors. Striving to define concepts in terms of quantifiable and measurable behaviors, social learning researchers place dominant consideration on methodology in their effort to be objective. Social learning theory is productive because it utilizes rigorous methods such as experimentation and objective data collection, and attempts to eliminate the least rigorous of methods such as purely subjective introspection. Since behavior is observable but inner experiences are not, social learning theorists reduce any and all experience to behavior that is specific and observable. Instruments for recording, measuring, and evaluating such behavior are also called operational definitions. Systems–interaction researchers have learned from social learning theory to emphasize method and to define communication behaviors operationally.

Like social learning theory, the systems–interactionist approach also recommends highly rigorous steps in the conduct of scientific inquiry. Generally these include stating the research problem, anticipating the obstacles to the solution of the problem, and devising ways and means to overcome the difficulties to provide a sound answer to the research problem. More specifically, these characteristic steps include constructing careful designs to facilitate objective observation and using complex, time-ordered designs to analyze and interpret the findings.

Cybernetics and Information Theories

Behavioral in orientation, the systems–interactionist approach was heavily influenced by theoretical developments in the study of communications that occurred toward the end of World War II. One of these developments was cybernetic theory (Gottman, 1979). At that time it was realized from the study of machine and animal behavior that feedback enabled adaptation to environmental changes. In addition, cybernetics proposed that feedback may result in circular relations between an individual and his or her environment as well as change that occurs when one gets feedback and responds by adjusting accordingly. Wiener (1948) provides as an example of feedback the way in which drivers may steer a car on an icy road:

> We . . . give to the steering wheel a succession of small, fast impulses, not enough to throw the car into a major skid but quite enough to report to our kinesthetic sense whether the car is in danger of skidding, and we regulate our method of steering accordingly. (p. 113)

Thus, cybernetic theory has made the systems–interactionists aware of the dynamic interplay between an individual and his or her environment, which includes the partner and the interplay among behaviors when couples engage in interaction and conflict.

The development of cybernetics coalesced in time with the development of information theory which is credited with viewing processes as stochastic, another concept that distinguishes the systems–interactionist paradigm from the others discussed in later chapters. In a stochastic process, the data for research take the form of a series of events that occur in a sequential pattern governed by probabilities of occurrence. The various subsequent events and their probabilities of occurrence given various antecedent events is known as stochastic probability. Shannon and Weaver (1949) presented the necessary mathematics (called information theory) for the analysis of stochastic processes in telecommunications.

To better understand the concept of stochastic probability, Fisher (1978) considers as an example a document typed in English:

> Certain letters occur so frequently in a pattern with other letters that we recognize them as words and are even able to decipher typographical errors because a particular letter does not "fit" the expected pattern. Even an omitted word, such as in the sentence "The bat _____ the ball" can be interpreted *within the probable pattern of the sentence* as a verb . . . such as *hit*. (p. 206)

Because of their interest in stochastic processes, information researchers theorized about the role redundancy. In real life, communication encounters noise (error, misunderstanding, or distortion). In communication generally, redundancy functions to overcome noise. Redundancy appears in communication as patterning whereby probabilities of preceding events constrain the probabilities of subsequent ones. If the probability of a pattern were

100% one could predict perfectly from any event what the next event would be.

Of course, human behavior is neither 100% nor zero redundant. An application of information theory's concept of the stochastic process to the study of the couples in conflict requires looking sequentially at exchanges of interpersonal messages and shifts in probabilities of response in one partner to the specific behavior of the other (Gottman, 1979). In the study of continuing reciprocal interactions in close, personal relationships, redundancy appears in a repeated pattern of interaction or style that gives a couple or a family its own individualized structure whether for better or for worse (Raush, Greif, & Nugent, 1979).

The concepts of feedback and stochastic process add to an understanding of how conflict escalates in intimate relationships. Because of the interdependent nature of behaviors during the conflict communication process (where antecedent behaviors influence the probabilities of subsequent behaviors), the systems–interactionist approach emphasizes behaviors that are linked to one another in an escalating, stochastic process.

General Systems Theory

To more adequately view human interaction, cybernetics and information theory were subsumed by a broader framework called general systems theory (von Bertalanffy, 1968). A common definition for *system* is *a set of interrelated components* acting together as a unit (Broderick & Smith, 1979). According to general systems theory, a system has some purpose—it is goal directed and adaptable. The system need not be aware or conscious that it has a goal, but the goal functions to direct activity toward its attainment. Able to adapt or reorganize itself on the basis of feedback about environmental changes, a system is controlled by its aims, a type of self-maintenance, or self-regulation. To restore homeostasis, changes in the environment fed back to the system create imbalances to which the system responds. Thus, the system maintains itself in pursuit of a goal. This aspect of system functioning is similar to the role played by a thermostat which exercises control over a system designed to heat a home or an office.

Systems–interactionists have learned from general systems theory the importance of interdependency. In general systems theory the interrelationship among the components in a system is more important than the components as individual entities. According to systems–interactionist researchers, the change from individuals to their interrelationships represents a paradigmatic shift that could be illustrated by a figure-ground reversal. Before general systems theory had an impact on behavioral researchers, an interpersonal relationship used to be seen as "background" with an individual as the "figure," but in the general systems approach, individuals recede into the background as the interpersonal relationship becomes the figure (Rogers, Millar, & Bavelas, 1985).

The application of general systems theory to conflict communication and intimacy emphasizes the whole, the overlap, or the area of commonality shared by communicators as partners. This holistic perspective views components of a system as a unit acting in concert. Since a couple's interrelationship consists of the mutual exchange of messages, systems–interactionist researchers view the couple as a communication system. They compare a couple's communication to a game where the move of one partner constrains the alternatives available to the other, thereby reducing uncertainty in predicting subsequent moves or plays. Moreover, since the discussion of issues, differences, or incompatibilities often includes the exchange of negative messages, a couple in conflict is also viewed as a communication system.

In the *Pragmatics of Communication*, Watzlawick et al. (1967) borrow heavily from general systems theory to view the behavior of couples and families as whole systems rather than mere collections of individuals. They suggest the following:

> A phenomenon remains unexplainable as long as the range of observation is not wide enough to include the context in which the phenomenon occurs. . . . If the limits of the inquiry are extended to include the effects of this behavior on others, their reactions to it, and

the context in which all this takes place, the focus shifts from the artificially isolated monad to the *relationship* between the parts of a wider system. (pp. 20–21)

Thus, the systems–interactionist paradigm views behavioral patterns and interpersonal relationships rather than particular behaviors or individuals in isolation. Partners' behaviors are understandable only when viewed in a behavioral context—in terms of an overall pattern or interpersonal relationship.

CONFLICT COMMUNICATION AND RELATIONSHIP SATISFACTION: SUPPORTING RESEARCH WITHIN A SYSTEMS–INTERACTIONIST APPROACH

Sources of Conflict: Behavioral Measures

Quite often a partner's behavior initiates the marital conflict process. From the systems–interactionist perspective, the sources of conflict are of interest for two reasons. First, sources of conflict refer to serious problematic behaviors, which fits the assumption that subsequent behaviors (i.e., conflict communication) are dependent on preceding behaviors. Therefore, one way to prevent or resolve conflict is to eliminate the behavior that leads to it, which makes it first necessary to identify the behavioral sources of conflict. Second, sources of conflict lead to the conflict behavior that researchers want to observe. Thus, another reason why the systems–interactionists are interested in identifying problematic behaviors is to use them to produce conflict in the laboratory.

These sources of conflict may be determined by asking partners to observe, record, and assess one another's behavior, which has the advantage of including one's definition of a partner's behavior that leads to conflict and one's reaction to it. While observing the families of "problem" children in the mid-1960s, researchers at a University of Oregon clinic noticed that these families appeared to be characterized by marital conflict, and so they began to focus on married couples and their interaction as a possible source for problematic behaviors in children. They created the Spouse Observation Checklist (SOC) (Wills, Weiss, & Patterson, 1974) to enable spouses to record daily their partners' behaviors that produced pleasure and displeasure (e.g., Birchler, Weiss, & Vincent, 1975). Originally, the SOC had seven categories of behavior: family recreation, meals and shopping, child care, finances, personal appearance, housekeeping, and transportation. For each category, about 15 specific behaviors were listed, each accompanied with a frequency rating and a degree of pleasing-ness–displeasingness rating. Normally, the researchers telephoned the spouses every 2 days for their reports. More recent versions of the procedure are computerized to reduce the lengthy checklist to those specific behaviors chosen by each spouse as important to his or her relationship satisfaction. The validity of the measures (the extent to which they are supported by objective evidence) is demonstrated by the different pleasing–displeasing ratios for dissatisfied and satisfied couples (4:3 and 29:7, respectively). The SOC also correlated with generally accepted measures of marital satisfaction (Weiss, Hops, & Patterson, 1973). Finally, as another important step in the study of marital conflict, couples' interactions were recorded for detailed analysis later (Hops, Wills, Patterson, & Weiss, 1972).

In an effort to generate conflict communication between spouses, Raush et al. (1979) devised a set of issues for couples to discuss. Raush et al. devised six laboratory interaction tasks that simulated conflict by requiring couples to role-play "common problem situations" from different viewpoints. The situations dealt with household responsibilities, leisuretime management, and husband–wife interpersonal distance. Because the couple's conversation was audiorecorded for later transcribing and coding, they were typically given 10 minutes to discuss each situation. Similarly, Strodtbeck's (1951) "revealed difference technique," which lists a number of potential differences, has been used to generate conflict communication in laboratory settings. These procedures have been criticized because couples differ in respect to the number of items on which they disagree (Olson & Ryder, 1970).

Since these potential issues and measures represented "best

guesses" by researchers, Gottman (1979) instituted the following procedure to identify problematic behaviors from tape-recorded marital interaction. Sixty couples who participated in a play-by-play interview that was audiotape-recorded produced 180 descriptions that were reviewed and reduced to 85 different "situations" that spanned 13 areas: money, sharing events of the day, in-laws, sex, religion, recreation, friends, alcohol/drugs, whether to have children, how to raise children, jealousy, household chores, and role definition. For purposes of convenience, Gottman regrouped the 85 different "situations" into 5 general topics representing potentially problematic behaviors.

Communication. These behaviors included spending time together, conversations, sharing feelings, recreation, and lifestyle.

Sex. These behaviors dealt specifically with physical affection, including manner, style, and frequency of sexual intercourse.

Jealousy. These behaviors occurred when a partner attended to other people of either sex.

In-law-relations. These behaviors included spousal differences in relating to one another's parents.

Chores. These behaviors included household maintenance, errands, management of children, and financial actions.

Gottman found that these types of behaviors, important to married couples generally, were especially problematic for many dissatisfied couples.

Efforts to determine the behaviors that partners find objectionable continue. Recently, Mead, Vatcher, Wyne, and Roberts (1990) assessed marital complaints and created a list of 29, including many problematic behaviors that are relevant to many dissatisfied couples:

Communication	Physical Abuse
Affection	Addiction
Sex	Power Struggles

Problem Solving	Finances
Health	Roles
Children	Individual Problems
Affairs	Household Duties
In-Laws/Relatives	Conventionality
Jealousy	Employment
Leisuretime	Alcoholism
Prior Marriage	Psychosomatic Illness
Friends	Loving Feelings
Personal Habits	Values
Religion	Expectations
Incest	

Mead and his colleagues found that summing scores over these problem areas differentiated satisfied from dissatisfied couples.

It is interesting to note that problematic behaviors may vary with stages of relationship growth or deterioration. According to Storaasli and Markman (1990), changes in clusters of problems appear between stages consistent with some changes in developmental tasks predicted by stage theories of family development. Moreover, men and women confront developmental tasks at different rates. Thus, one should not assume that the same behaviors are perceived as problems by both men and women and that different behaviors appear to be perceived as problems at different stages in relationship development.

Research suggests that intimate partners may confront or avoid conflict at different stages in *the life cycle* of their marriages. Using their own instrument designed for coding communication during interpersonal and marital conflict, Zietlow and Sillars (1988) found the following:

> *Young couples* tend to utilize an engagement style in which conflict issues are alternatively fought over, analyzed, and joked about. Younger partners are more likely to use a more direct and expressive style of communication than are older couples.

Middle-aged couples are avoiders. Occasionally, they are more similar to the younger couples when the discussion topics represent salient issues and frequently they are more similar to the older, retired couples when the issues are not salient. Suggesting low risk and disclosure, they have a noncommittal style of discussion that includes abstract remarks, irrelevant statements, and questions lacking focus.

Retired couples typically have a less expressive style for communication about sources of marital conflict than do young couples.

It would be interesting to know if young people tended to use the engagement style with other young people generally, if middle-aged people tended to avoid conflict with others their own age, and if retired people used a less expressive style for other retired people outside their primary relationship. Whether the duration of the marriage or the age of the partners is the key factor remains to be shown in future research. However, it appears that at different stages of one's life or a couple's life cycle, partners tend to deal differently with conflicts.

Observation and recording of the initiating behavior are important because it is linked to subsequent behaviors that are viewed in their entirety as conflict communication. Once the conflict is under way, behavioral interaction measures are useful for observing and recording the interrelated behaviors that occur during conflict and lead to escalation.

Conflict Communication: Behavioral Interaction Measures

As reported above, general systems theory's concern for the relationship rather than the individual spouse produced interest in overall patterns of couples' interaction. This interest resulted in the development of measures that represented streams of behavior over time.

Originally, it was thought that the category system developed by Bales (1950), Interaction Process Analysis (IPA), could be used to code a wide range of specific communication behaviors in families and couples. However, Raush, Barry, Hertel, and Swain (1974) report that the judgment of specific behaviors was too subjective, making it difficult to establish acceptable levels of reliability even among highly trained raters. Another coding scheme was Leary's (1957), which focused on two dimensions of interpersonal behavior, affection–hostility and dominance–submission (see Billings, 1979; Fineberg & Lowman, 1975). Like Bales's IPA, Leary's scheme assumed that all interpersonal behaviors could be classified into a few categories. Both systems were exhaustive in that coders must classify all behaviors in one category or another.

These coding schemes presented problems for researchers to overcome. To begin with, not all behaviors needed to be viewed as significant in conflict interaction. Theory was needed to distinguish important from unimportant verbal and nonverbal behaviors. Moreover, such methods were not entirely appropriate for assessing the interactions of intimate partners where affiliation and coercion were of greater range and more differentiated than either the Bales or Leary schemes accommodated (Raush et al., 1974).

To overcome these problems, Raush et al. developed a "six-category lumping scheme" (namely, cognitive, resolving, reconciling, appealing, rejecting, and coercive acts) for assessing audiotapes or written transcripts and wrote a useful manual for describing intimate couples' verbal communication. Rejection and coercion were viewed as negative affect messages because they led to prolonged and destructive conflict. By "lumping" verbal behaviors into six categories, researchers achieved 77 percent agreement among coders.

At about the same time, researchers at an Oregon clinic altered a family interaction coding scheme to assess changes in marital interaction by coding videotapes which resulted in the Marital Interaction Coding System (MICS) (Hops et al., 1972). Developed to provide sequential coding of couples' verbal and nonverbal behaviors during problem-solving discussions, the MICS, a behavioral observation measure, currently consists of 30 behavioral categories combined into 6 summary categories for scoring:

1. Problem-solving statements
2. Neutral statements
3. Positive statements
4. Negative statements
5. Nonverbal behaviors that facilitate communication
6. Nonverbal behaviors that impede communication

Coders who are trained to meet a standard of 70% reliability record data sequentially at 30-second intervals from the videotapes of couples' interactions. The coding of speech at timed intervals has been criticized as inappropriate because raters miss brief exchanges (especially facial expressions and vocal tone shifts) and count long exchanges more than once. Moreover, the researchers initially speculated over the interaction behaviors that are important in couples' problem-solving discussions. In spite of these limitations, the measure distinguishes satisfied from dissatisfied couples (e.g., Vincent, Weiss, & Birchler, 1975; Margolin & Wampold, 1981). Treatment studies also support the validity or objective value of the instrument as a behavioral interaction measure (e.g., Patterson, Hops, & Weiss 1975; Weiss et al., 1973). Extensive use has been made of this coding system, and many published reports are available.

Soon thereafter, Gottman (1979) developed the Couples' Interaction Scoring System (CISS). To represent affect (context) and content, the CISS coded separately nonverbal and verbal behavior, respectively. Coders who were unaware of the previous classification of satisfied or dissatisfied couples were trained separately to code videotaped interaction either for content or for affect, but not for both on the same couple. One rater would code the content of each "speech act" (a single complete thought unit) by assigning it to one of eight codes (disagreement, agreement, mind reading, communication talk, proposing a solution, summarizing other, summarizing self, feeling, or problem information). Another rater would code the affect of each behavior by assigning it to one of three codes (positive, negative, or neutral). Interestingly, with the exception of agreement, verbal behaviors (content codes) alone did not discriminate between previously classified dissatisfied and satisfied couples, although nonverbal behaviors (affect codes) alone did generally discriminate between the two types of couples.

Reliability figures for the CISS reported in the literature generally fall in the 80–90% range (Gottman, 1979); however, the use of agreement between observers has been criticized as an insufficient index (Gottman, 1979) because an overall agreement figure obscures the fact that some categories can be coded with higher accuracy than others where there may be little if any agreement among raters. Details on the CISS are available elsewhere (Gottman, 1979; Schaap, 1982).

Because the affect part of the CISS has been combined with other measures in subsequent research, it deserves more discussion. Gottman (1979) defines affect not as an inner emotional state but as certain communicator nonverbal behaviors. A communicator is said to deliver his or her message in a neutral, sarcastic, affectionate, or angry manner. As recommended by Mehrabian (1972), the affect coders are trained to scan first one partner and then the other for cues in the following order: face, vocal tone, body position, and movement.

Another measure of verbal behavior was developed by a group of psychologists. Viewing conflict interaction as an exercise in dominance, whereby spouses attempt to influence each other toward incompatible goals, Koren, Carlton, and Shaw (1980) deductively created four categories of verbal and nonverbal behavior.

> *Solution proposal.* Factual arguments, solution proposals (e.g., "Let's talk more often").
>
> *Criticism.* Critical comments (e.g., "You never listen to me").
>
> *Inquiry.* Seeking facts, opinions or feelings of the other (e.g., "What happened then?" "How do you feel about that?").
>
> *Responsiveness.* Conveying acknowledgement, agreement, or acceptance of the other's influence attempts (e.g., "I realize that." "I agree." "Let's do that."

Reliability among observers was found for the four categories of behavior: solution proposal (.94), criticism (.90), inquiry (.97), and responsiveness (.95). As for validity, however, only responsiveness and criticism discriminated between dissatisfied and satisfied couples.

During the 1980s, other schemes have been developed by communication researchers for coding conflict communication, especially verbal behavior, between intimates. One by Ting-Toomey is described here, while another by Sillars and his colleagues is the topic of the following section on conflict avoidance.

Based on the claim that verbal communicative acts are key determinants of marital satisfaction, Ting-Toomey (1983a, 1983b) provides the Intimate Negotiation Coding System (INCS) for measuring videotaped verbal interaction behaviors of an intimate couple when they hold different views on the same issue. The measure focuses on three types of verbal behavior: integrative (confirming, coaxing, compromising, and agreeing), disintegrative (confronting, complaining, defending, and disagreeing), and descriptive (socioemotional description and questions, task-oriented descriptions and questions).

Equipped with two video cameras to create a split-screen effect, Ting-Toomey (1983b) assigned spouses to sit facing one another and to discuss two problem-solving tasks for a total of 30 minutes. A total of 3,652 utterances were coded. Two experienced coders produced reliability between raters ranging from .86 to .89 and reliability from one coding to another by the same rater 3 weeks later ranging from .74 to .84. No measure of nonverbal communication behavior or communication behavior affect was included in this study.

Measuring Conflict Avoidance

Traditionally, research on conflict within the systems–interactionist paradigm favors conflict resolution and in turn direct confrontation (i.e., communication, discussion, or giving voice) rather than avoidance. This view is embodied in the belief that the only good conflict is a resolved conflict (Hawes & Smith, 1973). While Duck (1988) claims that not all conflicts are bad, he suggests that unresolved conflicts of certain types put couples on a collision course. Lloyd and Cate (1985) state that when couples are unable to resolve conflicts they feel bad about the issues and begin to develop doubts about each other that lead ultimately to disengagement. Lloyd (1990) finds that women who have broken up with their partners report fewer conflicts resolved previously than those who have not broken up.

Some studies have indicated that positive and constructive confrontation may resolve problems and restore intimacy and mutual satisfaction to a relationship. For example, seeing the partner's point of view results in resolving conflicts, which in turn produces greater marital satisfaction (Franzoi, Davis, & Young, 1985). In another example, Koren et al. (1980), who observed couples' interaction behaviors, attainment of resolutions, and satisfaction with outcomes, report that the nature of the interaction contributes to satisfaction or dissatisfaction. They claim that (1) one's responsiveness to a partner is associated with attainment of resolution of conflict and the partner's satisfaction with outcomes, (2) criticism of the partner is associated with the partner's dissatisfaction with outcomes and not with attainment of conflict resolution, and (3) the proposal of solutions predicts attainment of conflict resolution but not partners' satisfaction with outcomes.

It is not surprising that negative conflict behavior such as when a listener presents a "stone wall" to the speaker—not changing facial expressions or nodding the head, avoiding eye contact, or not offering brief vocalizations that tell the speaker that the listener is tracking—might do serious damage to an intimate relationship. Applied to marriage, this conflict behavior typically affects spousal satisfaction in the following two stages:

> The first stage begins with marital conflict in which the husband becomes very physiologically aroused and stonewalls with his wife. Then, finally, emotionally withdraws from the conflict. Over time he becomes overwhelmed by his wife's emotions and avoidant of any conflict with her.
>
> The husband's stonewalling is very aversive for the wife and leads to her physiological arousal. She responds by trying to re-engage her husband.

The second stage is marked by the withdrawal of the wife. She expresses criticism and disgust. Their lives become increasingly more parallel and he is fearful. In short, the husband's withdrawal from hot marital interaction is an early precursor of the wife's withdrawal. When both withdraw and are defensive, the marriage is on its way toward separation and divorce. (Gottman, 1991, p. 4)

The fact that couples can be trained to engage in more positive and constructive conflict communication enables them to resolve some conflicts and improve their intimate relationship. However, some scholars object to the idea of the absolute use of direct confrontation and the necessary resolution of conflict because avoidance of conflict may be useful at times. Support for this view is provided by Alberts (1990), who argues that in some situations one's partner or oneself cannot or should not change, and some way must be found for tolerating these differences. Intimates may avoid confronting issues through unconscious denial, distortion, misperception, consciously avoiding, and lying (Ryder & Goodrich, 1966; Strodtbeck, 1951). Because some issues cannot productively be resolved and some relationships are not sufficiently stable, committed, or involved to handle direct confrontation and conflict resolution, avoidance may be necessary for the functioning of long-term intimate relationships.

In fact, some communication researchers claim that some avoidance behaviors may actually enhance relationship or marital satisfaction. Sillars, Pike, Jones, and Redmon (1985) have created an interaction coding scheme as a measure of conflict communication that includes avoidance behaviors. They tape-recorded discussions of marital issues at the subjects' homes and later coded speaking turns in terms of verbal behaviors into 27 categories which were then collapsed into 3 general verbal ones:

Avoidance acts. Denial, noncontinuity, switching topics.
Distributive acts. Faulting, rejection, hostile statements.
Integrative acts. Information giving/seeking, description, disclosure, problem solving, support.

The overall percentage of agreement among coders was .94 in identifying the "acts," .89 for classifying verbal behaviors into the 27 codes, and .94 for categorizing the behaviors into the three general categories. To include nonverbal messages along with the verbal, Sillars and his colleagues also coded the interaction (from audiotapes) in terms of nonverbal affect by applying the vocal tone portion of Gottman's CISS. Use of the Sillars et al. instrument has revealed that some behaviorally coded avoidance behaviors are indeed associated with greater marital satisfaction (Pike & Sillars, 1985; Fitzpatrick, 1988).

Measuring Relationship Satisfaction

Researchers have discovered that one way to generate more scholarly interest in the topic of conflict communication behavior is to relate it to the topic of marital or relationship dissatisfaction. By distinguishing between satisfied and dissatisfied subjects, researchers are able to (1) observe patterns of conflict communication in both groups to determine whether they differ, and (2) measure changes from pretest (assessment) to posttest (reassessment) when evaluating the effectiveness of behavioral and marital therapeutic methods.

However, when researchers operating within the systems–interactionist perspective wish to separate satisfied from dissatisfied couples, they do so in a different manner from other researchers (e.g., cognitive–exchange; see Chapter 4). First, in keeping with a strong behavioral orientation, they may simply rely on a behavior indicator of marital dissatisfaction: For example, they may assume that couples who make appointments for marital therapy are dissatisfied with their relationship and that couples who are not seeking therapy are satisfied.

Second, they may use a self-report measure (e.g., paper-and-pencil tests that ask the respondent to report what he or she thinks, feels, or perceives) *if it correlates highly with behavioral measures* such as couples seeking marital therapy or interaction coding schemes. As argued above, the systems–interactionist approach relies heavily on objective behavioral measures, systematic controlled laboratory experiments, and quantified procedures. Yet, many researchers have found it convenient to incorporate into their studies a self-report instrument such as a subjective measure of relationship or marital satisfaction. Unlike other researchers (e.g., following the cognitive–exchange approach), researchers who hold to the systems–interactionist approach do not presume that cognition produces behavior.[1] They are using a quick and easy measure whose validity is supported by behavioral data.

The identification of satisfied and dissatisfied couples enables researchers to observe the pattern of conflict communication in both groups to determine if they differ and to ascertain how these differences relate to couples' overall assessments of their marriage or relationship. These findings are discussed in the next section.

Some Conflict Communication Differences Between Satisfied and Dissatisfied Couples

As described above, the systems–interactionist perspective views conflict as a form of dyadic communication which is classified as positive or negative by referring to its effects on the intimate nature of a couple's relationship. The overriding question in this line of research is how a couple can engage in conflict without doing (more) harm to the intimate relationship? Typical of more dissatisfied couples, negative conflict communication is defined as negative affect, coercive/controlling behavior, escalation, rigidity, and conflict avoidance.

Negative Affect

Systems–interactionists have learned from social learning theory to objectively measure conflict communication behavior. When engaged in conflict, dissatisfied couples rely more on a type of communication called negative affect (or punishing, aversive) messages. Moreover, these patterns are pervasive, invading even the couple's most mundane and frequent daily interactions. Dissatisfied compared to satisfied spouses deliver fewer reinforcers and more "punishers," and exhibit a lower ratio of reinforcers to punishers. Using the SOC (Weiss & Perry, 1983), several studies have discriminated between maritally dissatisfied and satisfied couples by computing pleases to displeases ratios or by computing the frequency of positive to negative affectional and instrumental interchanges (Barnett & Neitzel, 1979; Birchler et al., 1975; Margolin & Wampold, 1981).

Similar findings have been obtained from objective observation of conflict interaction behavior. Employing the MICS (Weiss & Summers, 1983), researchers have found that dissatisfied couples display higher rates of aversive behaviors (Birchler et al., 1975), express more criticisms/blame/accusations and are less responsive (Koren et al., 1980), and display fewer problem-solving behaviors and reinforcers (Vincent et al., 1975) than do satisfied couples. Obtaining data with the CISS, Gottman (1979) has observed that dissatisfied couples are more likely than satisfied couples to use cross-complaining and countercomplaints and less likely to engage in validation sequences (Gottman, Markman, & Notarius, 1977). After developing the INCS, Ting-Toomey (1983b) has discovered that, compared to satisfied couples, dissatisfied couples are more likely to begin a conflict by directly attacking one another with criticism and negatively loaded statements, followed by attempts to justify oneself and blame the other (Ting-Toomey, 1983a).

Again applying the separate content and affect coding structures of the CISS, Gottman et al. (1977) showed that affect codes rather than content codes discriminated marital distress. When monitoring spouses' physiological reactions during conflict, researchers found that physiological arousal was associated with marital dissatisfaction (Levenson & Gottman, 1983) and predicted marital dissatisfaction 5 years later (Levenson & Gottman, 1985).

Coercive/Controlling Behaviors

As argued above, systems–interactionists have learned from general systems theory to view couples and families as whole systems rather than mere collections of individuals. Researchers have revealed that coercive and controlling behavior during conflict interaction (as well as at other times) is associated with dissatisfying marital relationships. Partners who engaged in controlling behavior when resolving conflicts were more dissatisfied with their relationship than spouses who did not (Billings, 1979).

The intimate relationship often refers to a male–female relationship in which there appears to be sex differences in the use of controlling messages. According to Raush et al. (1974), women have learned to manipulate emotional communication better than men because they are traditionally a lower power group and more dependent on men. Raush and his colleagues say that whereas husbands appear to be more independent and supportive, their wives show more effects of coercion and make more appeals to their husbands from a position of lower power. However, Baker-Miller (1977) alleged that men use coercion in order to maintain control, whereas women (due presumably to lower status) attempt to make others happy to get their needs met. In conflict interactions that were behaviorally coded, husbands assumed a more coercive stance toward their partners, while women took an affiliative position (White 1989). Research on male–female nonverbal behavior (Mehrabian, 1972) showed that wives tended to behave in an inferior manner and were treated as inferior. Hawkins, Weisberg, and Ray (1980) found that wives reported that they wanted less controlling behavior from their husbands. Wives also reported that they wanted their husbands to be more vulnerable and share deeper, emotional intimacy. Thus, these studies favor the view that men are more likely to coerce and control others than are women.

Escalation: Negative Reciprocity

As discussed earlier, the general systems concepts of feedback and control have led systems–interaction researchers to examine conflict communication behaviors that are linked to one another in an escalating process. Once hostility is expressed by either partner, Gaelick, Bodenhausen, and Wyer (1985) show that it is likely to escalate in frequency over the course of the interaction. In both dissatisfied and satisfied couples, negative communication behavior is more likely to be reciprocated than positive (Gottman et al., 1977; Margolin & Wampold, 1981; Wills et al., 1974). Of course, there is greater negative reciprocity for dissatisfied couples than for happy ones (Gottman, 1982a, 1982b; Margolin & Wampold, 1981; Pike & Sillars, 1985).

Early research findings indicate that reciprocity of negative affect is symmetrical. However, Levenson and Gottman (1985) detail different types of negative affect messages which reveals that almost 78% of the husband's negative affect consists of anger and contempt, while only about 7% of the wife's negative affect is anger and contempt. Most of her negative affect is whining, sadness, and fear (about 93%). A husband may reciprocate his wife's anger, but she does not reciprocate his. Instead, the wife responds with fear to her husband's anger, suggesting a dominance structure and an asymmetry in sequential structure.

According to Gottman (1982a, 1982b), dissatisfied couples appear to respond verbally with complaints and criticism in the first conflict phase and nonverbally with hostile behaviors in the second phase. In the third phase, dissatisfied couples find it difficult to agree on a solution.

Rigidity

As discussed above, information is thought to flow from one person to another when a move by one partner constrains the alternatives available to the other, thereby reducing uncertainty in predicting subsequent moves or plays. Research shows that the interactions of dissatisfied couples show a higher degree of structure and more predictability of each spouse's behaviors than is found in the interactions of satisfied couples. Gottman (1979) reviews evidence of greater temporal predictability in the interactions of dissatisfied couples.

Conflict Avoidance

In addition to the negative, controlling, and aversive statements characteristic of heated disagreement, researchers have identified a number of verbal behaviors that comprise conflict avoidance. One way to manage a conflict is by teasing and using humor which are considered indirect methods for expressing unacceptable emotions on threatening or embarrassing topics. Because these methods serve to remind partners of their bonding, they can promote solidarity, reestablish intimacy, and excuse a slight. Not all jokes are equal, however. Alberts (1990) finds that benign humor consists of jokes about the self, about the relationship, or about the partner in a gentle manner. Hostile humor includes jokes about the partner in a negative way, particularly with sarcasm. Alberts also reports that more satisfied couples use humor not to resolve sources of conflict but to bring a verbal disagreement to an end on a playful note.

Other avoidance behaviors include denials of conflict, changing topics, contradictory statements about the presence of conflict, statements that direct the focus of conversation away from the conflict issues, and abstract, noncommittal, and indirect statements. Pike and Sillars (1985) found a strong reciprocity tendency in couples' interaction in that avoidance behaviors were typically followed by other avoidance behaviors. They also found that less satisfied couples engaged in fewer avoidance behaviors than more satisfied couples. Fitzpatrick (1988) reports that conflict avoidance in marriage as measured by the Sillars et al. (1985) instrument is a complex topic in that different types of married couples use conflict avoidance to different degrees and in different ways as either hostile or friendly.

There may be a difference in the way men and women engage in conflict and avoidance behavior. According to Gottman (1990), men show a larger ANS response to stress, respond more readily, and recover more slowly than do women. If extreme ANS response is viewed as harmful, unpleasant, and undesirable, then men might be more inclined than women to avoid situations that would be associated with repeated ANS activation. Thus, men may become more conciliatory and are likely to avoid conflict or terminate it by withdrawing.

Studies on male–female behavioral differences need to be conducted within the systems–interactionist paradigm. To date only limited support for differences exists. For example, Christensen and Heavey (1990) observed that both husbands and wives are more likely to be demanding when arguing over a change they want their partner to make, and more likely to be withdrawing when arguing over a change their partner wants in them. While neither sex indicated that it was more demanding than the other, data revealed that men overall were more withdrawn than women.

The systems–interactionist approach accounts for many empirical research studies on intimates in conflict. In addition to its productiveness as a research paradigm, it has also generated many useful techniques for helping couples improve their intimate relationship by encouraging positive conflict communication.

CONFLICT TRAINING: HELPING COUPLES RESOLVE ISSUES AND IMPROVE THEIR INTIMATE RELATIONSHIP

From a systems–interactionist perspective, anger and hostility are a breeding ground for verbal and sometimes physical abuse. Unfortunately, once spouses begin to use negative conflict communication behavior, they frequently discover that it is a powerful means to get a partner to comply. When both partners engage in such behaviors (negative reciprocity), conflict escalates. Thus, it is very important for couples to avoid, or dissipate, the early stages of anger.

Although the partners feel ambivalent about the personal compromises they perceive are required, many would like to resolve their differences but often do not know how. For this type of conflict, although real differences often exist, difficulties in self-expression and sensitivity to the partner usually exist as well. Improving couples' communication skills makes it possible for them to solve the real problems and negotiate differences. To enhance couples' abilities, education and training are needed to help them develop constructive attitudes and conflict communication skills.

Essentially, conflict training based on the systems–interactionist approach shifts from an emphasis on the individual to a view of the couple or family as a system in which the individual is only a part. This chapter elaborated on the holistic concepts of interdependence, relationship, and patterned behavioral interaction to show how behavior is understandable only in context. Consequently, the behavior of individual members is to be understood within the relationship or interpersonal system (defined as the way partners interact with one another). If change is to occur, it must be brought about in the system as a whole or in the way partners interact with each other. This shift in perspective is realized through a variety of techniques.

Behavior Modification

Some behaviors lead to more positive outcomes than others—that is, some behaviors deescalate emotional outbursts. To prevent the escalation of conflict and to restore homeostasis, deescalation behaviors need to be identified and encouraged. For example, discussion that focuses on resolving a problem is less emotionally upsetting than name calling and partner blame. Thus, the couple as an interpersonal system may redirect itself in pursuit of a more positive and constructive goal. As pointed out earlier, this aspect of system functioning is similar to the role played by a thermostat. To accomplish this goal, conflict training within the systems–interactionist approach reinforces positive behaviors but not negative behaviors. In 1972, Liberman described a simple program in behavioral modification that consisted of only four steps:

1. Initial assessment to identify positive and negative behaviors;
2. Treatment through restructuring the conflict communication behavioral exchange by altering partners pattern of responses to each other;
3. Maintenance; and
4. Follow-up through periodic reassessment.

Through the use of reciprocal behavioral contracts (quid pro quo contracting—giving something and getting something in return), special days (e.g., with a higher than usual positive-negative ratio), and imitative learning techniques (e.g., modeling and rehearsal through role playing), forces may be set in motion that favor positive reciprocity (Falloon & Lillie, 1988).

> In modeling, the trainer plays the role of one of the spouses (who watches) and interacts with the partner.
>
> Rehearsal is a procedure whereby more desirable responses to conflict situations are practiced under the supervision of the trainer.
>
> Immediately following behavioral rehearsal, partners should be reinforced socially by encouraging comments.
>
> The trainer should also coach the partners by providing rewards and punishments for specific behaviors during the rehearsals and at other times.

Also, explicit or implicit contracts develop as couples interact. These verbal agreements consist of new behaviors to be substituted for old ones. A contract should make apparent how it is to be modified when needed. During behavior modification training, a couple may make explicit the terms of the contract, or in their own interaction, create new ways in which each partner is expected to act toward the other. In either case, in renegotiating and verbalizing new relationship agreements, problematic behaviors must be made explicit and changed in conformity with the agreement. Jacobson (1978) has found that behavioral contracting methods produced fewer negative behaviors compared to the control groups.

Communication Skills Training

In addition to behavioral modification, research has shown that training in conflict communication skills enhances the effectiveness of couples' training (Gottman, 1979). In many systems–interactionist-oriented programs, the teaching of effective conflict communication skills is directed toward enhancing intimacy within the marital relationship. Common problems of conflict communication targeted for treatment by skills training exist at two levels: the concrete verbal and nonverbal behaviors making up an interaction and metacommunication-level behaviors that structure the interaction and provide for the adaptation and change of that structure (Stuart, 1980).

Concrete or specific verbal and nonverbal behaviors convey either interest or disinterest or warmth or coldness, as well as attraction or repulsion. As small as changes in behaviors may be, they may subsequently make drastic changes in a couple's pattern of interaction. Microanalysis of interaction behavior has the power to shape partners' impressions of one another, their expectations for future interaction, and their satisfaction with the relationship. By observing their own conflict behavior on audio/videotape, partners may better observe these details. Various instruments exist (e.g., Gottman, 1979; Hops et al., 1972) to help trainers identify specific negative and positive verbal and nonverbal behaviors. Gottman, Notarius, Markman, et al. (1976) provide a "table talk" exercise that permits spouses to code ongoing conflict communication. Jacobson and Margolin (1979) describe a number of ways in which couples may record their partner's "pleasing" and "displeasing" behaviors on a daily basis (using, for example, the SOC described earlier).

To operate at a metacommunication level from a systems–interactionist perspective, the trainer attempts to "break frame" with the couple's punctuation of events, accusations, and defenses and instead calls attention to the couple's recurring and problematic interaction patterns (Buttny, 1990). When conflicting partners are trained to analyze and discuss their interaction behavior, they are behaving at a metacommunication level.

Gottman, Notarius, Gonso, and Markman (1976) present details, materials, and exercises for a couple's marital enhancement program that consist of training in five conflict skills that reflect the communication and metacommunication levels.

Listening and validation. Specifically, the listening skills taught are checking-out and paraphrasing. A validation skill is also included to increase the frequency of "accepting" behaviors, such as assent and agreement when a partner is expressing feelings. For example, a partner learns to say, "I can see how you feel about that now."

Leveling. To reduce blaming, mind reading is discouraged in favor of more positive statements. Partners are trained to say, "When you do this or say that or . . . I feel . . . (e.g., threatened, bad, angry, unwanted).

Editing. Couples are taught how to "edit" the scripts of other couples. This feedback teaches them to be more positive and considerate toward one another.

Negotiating. A family meeting is used as a device for creating a contract and turning ambiguous negative gripes into specific positive, constructive suggestions.

Revealing hidden agendas. Partners are encouraged to make explicit previously unstated issues relating to closeness, affect, responsiveness, and power.

Jacobson (1977) tested the effectiveness of communication skills training by randomly assigning couples to experimental and control groups. Using the behavioral observation measure known as the MICS, he found that the group receiving training decreased from pretest to posttest in negative categories on the MICS and increased in the positive categories, while there was no change for the control group.

Through positive conflict communication training, which includes awareness of warning signs, metacommunication and concrete communication skills, and contracts, couples may regain intimacy.

CONCLUSION

Due to the influence of social learning theory, one of the major methodological breakthroughs in the study of couples in conflict is the development by systems–interactionist researchers of objective and reliable observational methods (coding schemes) for coding audiotaped or videotaped interaction between partners. This approach not only emphasizes behavioral observation but also is committed to the social learning theory concepts of data quantification, testability, and replication.

Thanks also to the influence of cybernetic, information, and general systems theories, systems–interactionists have identified, defined, and applied a number of useful concepts to the study of couples in conflict. As components of a system interact with one another, they obtain feedback and continually adjust themselves to conform to a familiar pattern. Applied to the study of conflict between intimates viewed as a couple or a system, the concept of feedback offers an explanation for a familiar pattern of communication behavior that involves negative reciprocity—the reciprocation of displeasurable behaviors—commonly known as escalating conflict.

Since a system's parts or components are interdependent, the relationship among the components becomes more important than the individual components themselves. This holistic perspective views the partners as a unit acting in concert (i.e., a relationship) and is an entirely different view from that of either individual. This shift in perspective makes one realize that some subsequent behaviors result from the relationship or initial behaviors. What goes on between people is actual behavior constrained by the nature of their previous behavioral pattern or relationship.

The systems–interactionists' concern for the relationship rather than the individual spouse or family member focuses on redundancy—repeated patterns of couples' interaction. In the study of continuing reciprocal interactions in close personal relationships, redundancy appears in a repeated pattern of interaction that gives a couple its own structure whether for better or for worse. This interaction pattern of interdependent behaviors or stochastic process becomes the relationship. Therefore, to change the relationship, a couple must change its conflict communication pattern.

Systems must be able to reorganize themselves on the basis of information received (feedback) about environmental changes. Changes in the environment fed back to the system create imbalances to which the system responds to restore homeostasis. Thus, the system maintains itself in pursuit of a goal. When the goal is negative, for example, a couples' interaction functions to harm the intimate relationship, then cues must be recognized so that harmful behaviors are taken out of behavioral sequence and beneficial ones are enacted.

The benefits of the systems–interactionist approach as a research paradigm have their price. For one, the behavioral observation schemes are labor and cost intensive. Gottman (1979) reports that in addition to the time first spent training coders, it takes approximately 20 hours to code 1 hour of videotaped interaction. Thus, learning to code is usually a "grueling and frustrating" experience.

When collecting data from couples in conflict, confidentiality must be maintained. When audio- and videotaping a couple's interaction, researchers should use legal consent forms. They should indicate to the subjects the specific uses of the videotape, secure permission from those they videotape, and ensure that the tapes are not replayed for other purposes. The rights of human subjects are an important area that deserves strict attention by researchers.

In sum, the systems–interactionist approach focuses on couples' actual conflict communication and strives to enhance intimacy in their relationship by encouraging more positive interaction patterns. The fact that this approach has emerged as a popular paradigm for analyzing actual conflict communication behavior in intimate relationships does not mean that it is the only one possible. It is, however, a credible research paradigm, and it accounts for a large number of empirical studies on conflict, many of which have contributed greatly to a better understanding of conflict in intimate relationships. It is, however, necessary to adopt a different approach to better understand the process of conflict in divorce mediation which is the topic of the next chapter.

NOTE

1. Gottman and Levenson (1986) and Margolin, Michelli, and Jacobson (1988) report that there are a number of acceptable self-report measures of

marital satisfaction, such as the Marital Adjustment Scale (MAS) (Locke & Wallace, 1959) and the Dyadic Adjustment Scale (DAS) (Spanier, 1976), that are often used by researchers to identify satisfied and dissatisfied couples (Margolin, 1990). The MAS, which used to be the most popular, has yielded some of its popularity to the DAS.

The DAS includes 32 items regarding such topics as the sharing of outside interests, the extent the couple agrees on family finances, religious matters, and how often the spouses kiss each other. Originally, Spanier indicated the existence of four factors underlying the items: dyadic cohesion, dyadic satisfaction, dyadic consensus, and affectional expression, but more recently, researchers have found only the first three (Margolin et al., 1988).

How does one interpret a score from the DAS? Spanier (1976) provides norms for spouses in general ($\overline{X}$ = 114.8, SD = 17.8) and for divorced partners in particular ($\overline{X}$ = 70.7, SD = 23.8), but not for dissatisfied spouses who are still married. To identify this latter group, Margolin (1990) recommends a cutoff at one standard deviation below the married sample mean, at a score of 97.0. Following Baucom and Mehlman's (1984) finding that a score from the more dissatisfied spouse is a better predictor of future marital status than is the average of both spouses' scores, Margolin uses the score from the least satisfied spouse to distinguish dissatisfied from satisfied couples. This method also makes use of the discovery that wives and husbands function quite differently in marriage (Fineberg & Lowman, 1975; Floyd & Markman, 1983). Along with the DAS, Margolin uses other measures of marital satisfaction and spouses who respond to newspaper or radio announcements as a first step toward obtaining counseling.

THREE THE RULES–INTERVENTIONIST PERSPECTIVE ON DIVORCE MEDIATION

Ending relationships based on love is hard. Most people need a little help from their friends, family, or therapist, if they can afford one. Sometimes they seek amicable future relationships with their ex-partners and sometimes they seek revenge. Often people don't know for sure what they want.

If the couple is married, the law requires them to continue looking after their children, however they feel about each other. The law also attempts a fair settlement of the financial and property relationships that are ended with the divorce.

In the 1980s, divorce mediation has become another option for working through the emotional and legal issues in ending a marriage. . . . In mediation, an impartial third party assists people in a dispute to identify and communicate their grievances and interests to each other and helps them to negotiate their own settlements.

(Chandler & Chandler, 1987, p. 123)

Rules–interventionists define conflict as mediation in which a neutral third party assists divorcing partners in the process of resolving their dispute (Allen & Donohue, 1987). Divorce mediation is one case in which intimates or previously intimate partners may participate in a formal negotiation process. The rules–interventionists' view of conflict emphasizes the development of reciprocal arguments and counterarguments and proposals and counterproposals (Sawyer & Guetzkow, 1965) in quest of a "zone of reasonable" outcomes for both parties (Putnam & Jones, 1982). This implies a great deal of give-and-take. Teachman and Polonko (1990), using data from a national study on mediation, found evidence that divorcing parents make trade-offs between several dimensions related to their children, including custody, visitation, child support, and the marital property.

Milne (1986) claims that mediation is a "contracting process" that serves to reduce irrationality by preventing personal recriminations and focusing on the dissolution of the marriage and resolving disputes. In mediation, divorcing partners are ending one relationship and beginning another; that is, they close down its old form and transform it to a new shape. A contemporary view of divorce has produced a need for redefining the experience from one of dissolving the family to one of restructuring it and for creating relationships in which former spouses can cooperate with each other (on matters such as custody and visitation) long after the divorce (Grebe, 1988).

The notion of conflict as divorce mediation may seem novel to some researchers who are accustomed to thinking of "mediation" primarily as a means by which a third party resolves issues to restore an otherwise failing relationship. However, even though opportunities for interaction may be limited, divorcing partners engage in disputes that require exchanging information, developing mutual agreements, and influencing one another. In addition, divorcing partners appear to be as rich a resource on conflict between intimates as other couples who are married or romantically involved. Finally, divorce mediation is rapidly becoming an alternative to the courts. For these reasons, it is a topic of interest that is attracting an increasing number of scholars.

Because divorce mediation presents an entirely different context or type of relationship from dyadic conflict communication as discussed in the previous chapter, theory and research about divorce mediation appear to need a different approach (e.g., Spanier & Thompson, 1983; Thompson & Spanier, 1983). The rules–interventionist approach is particularly useful for studying conflict in divorce mediation because it is designed for three interacting individuals—the divorcing partners and the intervening third-party mediator—and each person's effect on the outcome of the mediation process. The introduction of the mediator as an interventionist emphasizes the partners' inability to resolve disputes by themselves and the need for considering interests above their own. Unlike the systems–interactionist approach, where stochastic probability governs the outcome of interaction, in the rules–interventionist approach, the mediator intervenes to place interaction under the control of rules. This helps the mediator achieve a more successful outcome of the mediation process rather than letting the spouses' interaction alone determine the outcome.

Although the rules–interventionist approach guides some researchers who gather empirical data on divorce mediation, it is not as popular a research approach as the others discussed in this book, which are more generally recognized as paradigms of inquiry. Thus, it might seem unusual to devote an entire chapter to it. It is believed by some, however, that the rules–interventionist approach is implicit in the nonempirical research conducted in the past on divorce mediation and is rapidly becoming the dominant paradigm for the conduct of empirical research on divorce mediation in the future.

BACKGROUND

Compared to private conflicts that tend to occur in the privacy of one's own home or involve only the partners themselves, conflict of this type is seen more as a social, public, and cultural event. An understanding that defines the relationship and governs interaction may be created by a couple over time, but during divorce this understanding may no longer hold, resulting in a breakdown in communication. The addition of an interventionist to the divorce process provides an opportunity for the mediator and society to fill the vacuum with socially approved rules that redefine the couple's relationship and create new patterns of communication.

Divorce Mediation Theory: Divorce Mediation Presuppositions and Assumptions Compared to Those of Adjudication

In an effort to formulate the foundation for a comprehensive theory of mediation, Taylor (1981) described several basic presuppositions.

1. People avoid negative experiences and pain.
2. People make better decisions when integrating feelings and decisions without becoming irrational.
3. People make better decisions for themselves (i.e., through mediation) than do outsiders (e.g., courts and judges).
4. People are more likely to support agreements if they take part in formulating them.
5. Trained mediators are necessary to help guide people through mediation.
6. The mediation process remains the same from one divorce to another, but substantive issues vary.
7. History of the relationship plays a limited role in mediation.
8. Agreements tend to last when they reflect the interests of the parties involved.

Moreover, Lerman (1984) discussed several assumptions underlying divorce mediation. First, it is assumed that both partners must share responsibility for the failure of the marriage; so mediation efforts are not directed toward determining who is at fault, whether conduct is criminal, or who is to blame. Thus, mediation usually requires the withdrawal of any criminal charges previously brought against one another. Moreover, records are confidential, attorneys are prohibited from representing either spouse's interests during mediation, and any information shared during mediation may not be used later in court.

Second, mediation is considered closely aligned with a view of the family as a complex, private system and as a delicate entity that must be respected even in matters of divorce. Therefore, it is assumed that spouses are in the best position to decide for themselves with minimal intervention by others. This assumption is clearly stated by other researchers:

> This notion, that mediators regulate procedure without affecting content, is a common theme in writing about mediation programs. The working assumption in mediation is that the procedure should empower disputants to resolve their own dispute, not that the procedure should substitute informal authority for formal authority. Mediators create the conditions in which the two disputants can work together to reach a consensus solution to a problem, while minimally influencing the alternatives considered or the agreement reached. (Jacobs, Jackson, Hallmark, Hall, & Stearns, 1987, p. 291)

Thus, divorcing partners determine issues and decisions, but the mediator makes sure that rules regarding interaction patterns are observed.

Third, it is assumed that mediation is more humane than other alternative means of resolving conflicts between divorcing partners. The idea is to completely remove divorce cases from the law-enforcement system. Thus, mediation is offered as an alternative to adjudication.

Fourth, it is assumed that all issues are resolvable. In addition, no position is explicitly labeled irrational or unreasonable. Thus, mediation respects the views of both spouses but encourages compromise, cooperation, and mutual understanding.

Mediation and the assumptions underlying it are better understood when compared with an alternative form of marital-divorce dispute resolution: adjudication. Most obviously, adjudication or litigation differs from mediation in that the roles of lawyers and judges are key in the courtroom. As Girdner (1985) observes, in adjudication, the disputing parties "yield their right to make the decisions to a third party who imposes a decision upon them" (p. 34). When the parties yield their decision-making power to the judge, they lose some influence over the process (unless they agree to return to mediation or otherwise attempt to settle out of court). Because adjudication is usually in the public domain, the judge represents the interests of the state, and presumably the parties' interests are rendered less important than in mediation.

In contrast to mediation, adjudication starts out as a form of competition and remains so, or gets worse (Werner, 1990). According to the American Bar Association's 1981 *Moral Code of Professional Responsibility*, the attorney is required to represent only his or her client since the assumption is that the other partner is represented by opposing legal counsel (Kaslow, 1984). Initially, the parties retain the services of attorneys who are trained in the adversary role. Pitting one client against the other, the attorneys "translate" the information and presentations to conform to the standards of the court. For example, "the evidentiary rules are categories which function to regulate and organize the content of the information presented in the court" (Girdner, 1985, p. 37). Because the rules of procedure dictate the adversarial structure of the legal proceedings, the attorneys structure and organize the information to convince the judge that their party's position is the right one. Due to the adversarial nature of the process, Girdner (1985) claims that court-imposed decisions may actually perpetuate conflict between the parties. Kaslow (1984) adds:

> Sometimes the battle becomes hostile and demeaning, resulting in prolonged bitterness and anguish into which relatives and friends are drawn; children are traumatized by the continuing strife . . . and everyone involved suffers a long-term loss of self-esteem and confidence. (p. 62)

Many mediators recommend that divorcing partners do not seek advice from lawyers when engaged in mediation. Obviously lawyers are the product of legal training. In their attempts to influence a judge, the lawyers as representatives of their clients may tend to polarize them, a process that pulls partners further apart. Even outside the courtroom, lawyers often emphasize a win–lose outcome and push their particular client to win every possible advantage, regardless of the possible effect on the other party (Haynes, 1981).

The theoretical differences between mediation and adjudication are realized in actual differences in ex-spouse compliance defined as the degree to which participants abide by the terms of their settlements (Burrell et al., 1990).

Research reveals that mediated agreements produce more compliance than court-imposed settlements. In a 2-year follow-up study of divorced couples, Bahr (1981) found that only 10% of the mediated couples returned to the court with problems related to custody or visitation, compared to 26% of the couples who sought adjudication or litigation. Bahr, Chappell, and Marcos (1987) interviewed 36 couples who participated in divorce mediation. They discovered that 20 were able to reach agreement in child custody disputes and that those who participated in mediation achieved a greater happiness than those who did not participate. Bautz and Hill (1989) sent questionnaires to randomly selected divorced residents of New Hampshire. Of the 120 usable responses (52 litigation; 68 mediation), the following results were obtained:

Mediation parties were more likely to select joint legal custody than parties who choose litigation.

Ninety-seven percent of those couples who used mediation made all child support payments, missing none. A significantly higher proportion of the litigation group, 37%, reported late or no child support payments.

Mediation couples were significantly more satisfied with the final divorce agreement than couples who litigated. Most (70–90%) said they were satisfied with the process and would recommend it.

Mediation couples had a more harmonious or cordial relationship after the divorce than couples who chose to litigate.

Couples who used mediation more often described their divorce settlement as being very to somewhat fair, while traditional couples were more likely to report, somewhat fair to very unfair.

These findings supported those obtained by Pearson (1981) and literature reviews by Emery and Wehr (1987) and Kressel (1987).

Although strong evidence existed for the superiority of mediation to adjudication for custody and visitation disputes (Sprenkle & Storm, 1983), many attorneys interviewed took the position that divorce mediation was not successful (Bahr et al., 1987).

Rules Theory and Normative Force

As indicated above, rather than let the interaction alone determine the outcome of a dispute, mediators are trained to create and enforce rules to give the mediator greater control over the outcome of the interaction. In theory, rules define social relationships and regulate social interaction (Cahn, 1987). Rules are defining because they affect the way couples view their relationship. Members of a culture share a common set of rules or expectations regarding friendship, courtship, marriage, or other intimate relationships (Argyle & Furnham, 1983; Harre & Secord, 1972). Part of the divorcing process requires acceptance of a nonintimate relationship by previously intimate partners and acceptance of a restructured parental relationship (not its destruction).

In addition, as guides to action, rules may also regulate interaction and many other human actions when they function as criteria for choice among alternative messages and other behaviors. It is not unique to include choice in the paradigm, but it is the case that normative expectations rather than causal (see Chapter 4 for a causal model) or stochastic processes (see Chapter 2) provide the rules–intervention approach with a unique structure for making predictions. When studying the nature of actions, rules–interventionists argue that often it is impossible to identify causes, effects, and causal relationships. When actions occur, one may not observe a physical change that functions as a stimulus or cause, and nothing may appear to function as a response or effect. Because actions fail to conform to causal laws, many human actions are described as arbitrary, learned, and often unpredictable. They require normative explanations.

Like guideposts, regulative rules are normative in contrast to the causal force of laws because they indicate what should be done (Cushman & Whiting, 1972). A rule exists when people perform the same actions under certain conditions because each expects the others to so behave, and each is aware of the others' expectations. Thus, a pattern of behavior is said to be rule governed when mutual expectations exist regarding what is appropriate in a given situation. A rule or standardized usage, then, is prescriptive and serves as a criterion for evaluating the appropriateness of intentional behavior. Although rules are social conventions, which can be violated or changed by individuals or groups, it is argued that when people know the rules, they tend to conform to them.

Analytically, regulative rules take the form of practical reasoning: X intends to bring about Z; X considers that in order to bring about Z, he or she must do Y; and, therefore, X sets out to do Y (von Wright, 1971). It is argued that there exists a class of human behaviors governed by a particular set of rules and that persons have some degree of choice among alternative behaviors and rule sets, monitor and critique their performance, and act in response to normative forces.

By including choice, rules, and normative forces, rules–interventionists view mediation as a structured social activity guided and defined by rules designed to convert competitive orientations and actions into cooperative ones. According to Allen and Donohue (1987):

> Successful mediators lay down rules at the beginning of the session. . . . The rules enforced by the mediator go beyond explaining the legal status of the mediator and mediation. The mediator also establishes rules for behavior during the session. The mediator limits the agenda for the session and the tone of the discussion. If disputants decide to call each other names and dwell on the issues causing the divorce, the mediator can and does exercise the option to ask the disputants to stop discussing those issues or change their use of language. . . . Unsuccessful or less skilled mediators seem hesitant or unwilling to enforce rules of behavior during the sessions. (p. 280)

It may be no accident that even early practice in divorce mediation was based on a rules approach (Coogler, 1978). Rules such as the ones listed by Allen and Donohue define and enforce empowerment, consideration of the best interests of all family members, full and honest disclosure of assets, cooperative problem solving, and equitable distribution of assets. Structured mediation gains support from the work of Deutsch (1973), who claimed that "it is evident that conflict can be limited and controlled by institutional forms . . . social roles . . . rules for conducting negotiations . . . and specific procedures" (p. 377). Grebe (1988) adds that "structured mediation is a means of limiting conflict through the use of rules for the negotiations and by specific procedures to encourage open communication" (p. 229).

Intervention Theory: The Role of the Mediator as an Interventionist

The incorporation of an impartial third party in mediation introduces the concept of intervention. Interventionist roles vary according to how much control a mediator exercises over the mediation process and how much the mediator gets involved in it (Donohue et al., 1989).

The mediator may be viewed as "an impartial third party who has no authoritative decision-making power" (Burrell et al., 1990, p. 105). In contrast, the parties may have expectations about the role of the mediator such as expecting her or him to solve their problems for them. From their perspective, an interventionist is needed because they believe they cannot resolve the issues by themselves. Although mediators vary in the amount of control they exercise over structuring the course of interaction between the parties, they need to inform the partners that they have no authoritative decision-making power and may only structure the interaction, serve as a resource person, and help the disputants reach their own agreement.

One of the most important roles of the mediator is to encourage cooperation and discourage competition between divorcing partners.

Encouraging Cooperation Rather Than Competition

Essentially, a mediator's objective is to create a cooperative environment for the parties to discuss emotional and substantive issues and reach agreement (Barsky, 1983; Jones, 1988; Kiely & Crary, 1986; Kolevzon & Gottlieb, 1983; Weiss, 1976).

The process of divorce mediation is successful to the extent that it moves from a competitive to a cooperative orientation. Beck and Beck (1985) view competition as a defensive communication climate and cooperation as supportive. Competitive orientation involves a completely different set of actions in which one gains at the expense of others and such mental states as descensus or disagreement. Beisecker (1970) defines competitive communication as self-promoting because it serves as a vehicle through which individuals attempt to distort the other's perceptions of the situation in order to obtain an advantage. A cooperative orientation consists of actions characteristic of organized action (e.g., working together) and a thought process known as consensus (e.g., shared understanding, actual agreement). It also facilitates attempts to discover areas of common interest regarding issues (Beisecker, 1970).

Divorce mediation sessions usually begin with a broad and confused discussion of issues seen from competitive orientations, but when successful, proceed to more detailed and specific statements out of which cooperation and consensus (shared meanings) may emerge to facilitate and clarify final recommendations and actions.

Representing Social Concerns

Mediators attempt to help partners create agreements that are reasonable. As a mediator moves the divorcing couple from competition to cooperation, he or she attempts to create conditions for rational discussion by the divorcing partners. Conflict resolution takes on a unique character in divorce mediation because it is governed by the need for the mediator to establish "a zone of reasonableness."

In addition, mediators adhere to certain social values and

represent society's concerns regarding the matter of divorce. For example, since children under the age of 18 are involved in a majority of divorces, mediators find that the greatest social concern regarding the impact of divorce is its effect on the children (Long & Forehand, 1990; Veltkamp & Miller, 1988).

Rule Setting and Enforcement

Structured mediation is based on Deutsch's (1973) principles of conflict resolution (Coogler, Weber, & McKenry, 1979). Deutsch (1973) lists eight conditions that produce adherence to rules in negotiation.

1. The rules are known.
2. The rules are clear, unambiguous, and consistent.
3. The rules are not perceived to be biased against one's own interests.
4. The other adheres to the rules.
5. Violations are quickly known by significant others.
6. There is significant social approval for adherence and significant social disapproval for violation.
7. Adherence to the rules has been rewarding in the past.
8. One would like to be able to employ the rules in the future. (pp. 379–380)

By meeting Deutsch's eight criteria, rules like the ones presented by Allen and Donohue (1987) make it easier for mediators to help divorcing partners, as naive negotiators, to mediate effectively and fairly. The rules of structured mediation enable inexperienced partners to negotiate on a more equal footing and to restructure their lives at a time of emotional and economic crisis. Moreover, the chances of surprises and the uncertainty that can exacerbate emotional conflict are avoided or reduced. Perhaps for these reasons, the structured mediation model has been in use longer than any other method developed for divorce mediation (Grebe, 1988).

Mediator Communication Competence

To select the appropriate intervention techniques for creating a cooperative environment for reaching agreement, the mediator must also be competent in communication. According to Cooley and Roach (1984), communication competence refers to "the knowledge of appropriate communication patterns in a given situation and the ability to use the knowledge" (p. 25). Donohue, Allen, and Burrell (1985) add to an understanding by suggesting that the competent communicator "is aware of the communication rules that a particular speech community uses to interpret a specific sequence of events" (p. 76).

An important part of the mediator's role is to teach the divorcing spouses to be more competent in communication. Mediators have discovered that many couples who enter divorce mediation have found it difficult to communicate, relate, and work with each other in the past. Moreover, both men and women rank communication problems highest of 18 perceived causes of divorce (Cleek & Pearson, 1985). Thus, the mediator must help the couple build confidence in the mediation process, find common ground, and communicate effectively.

Counseling Role

Even with the increase in no-fault divorces, marital dissolution is often accompanied by emotional pain and suffering: anger, fear of separation, a sense of failure and loss of self-esteem, and feelings of guilt. Kressel, Jaffee, Tuchman, Watson, and Deutsch (1980) have found that typically one spouse is likely to desire divorce more than the other. One implication of this observation is that those who are not taking the initiative may have less time to prepare for the emotional and substantive issues in the divorce. Favoring dependence on others, some divorcing spouses may need help dealing with their new sense of autonomy. There is a need to establish a new social identity as a single, formerly married person, a new economic identity based on fewer resources, and a new psychological identity that is likely to have suffered rejection by other people (Stuart & Jacobson, 1986/1987).

The emotional trauma that frequently accompanies divorce raises the question: Should mediators be therapists? Haynes (1981) argues that the marital therapist is in the best position to make the separation and divorce as painless as possible, to help the couple develop new identities, and to assist the children to make the transition by reducing the conflict typical of divorce. Haynes claims that the decision to divorce is not the beginning of a new process but a point on "the continuum of a dissolving marriage." According to Haynes, "The therapist who has been helping the couple up to this point is better informed about the total picture . . . and would be more able to use the knowledge to facilitate the divorce" (p. 4).

Some argue against using a therapists as mediator. First, while the role of the therapist is similar to that of the mediator in that he or she is expected to create a controlled climate that encourages clients to express their desires and discuss problems constructively, the roles are different in that therapists are expected to achieve insight rather than to replace conflict action with reconciliation to reach a settlement (Stuart & Jacobson, 1986/1987). Second, one could argue that the goal of therapy is to repair the marital relationship rather than renegotiate it into a divorce (Markowitz & Engram, 1983). As Rice and Rice (1986) point out, many couples enter marital therapy as a "last-ditch attempt" to save a marriage. Some therapists measure their success as therapists by how many couples they see stay together. Thus, the goal of many marital therapists is more to preserve rather than help dissolve the marriage.

Analysis of the divorce mediation process is aided by knowledge of the role of a third party as mediator. It is time to review the research on the effects of different mediator communication behaviors on the divorce mediation process.

DIVORCE MEDIATION: SUPPORTING RESEARCH WITHIN A RULES–INTERVENTIONIST APPROACH

The identification of mediator actions and the factors that affect outcomes of mediation are complicated by the fact that the data are not dyadic in nature but triadic, involving divorcing partners and a mediator. This orientation to research has resulted in unique sources of conflicts and conflict interaction patterns that separate settled disputes from unsettled ones.

Sources of Conflicts

There is a difference between the sources of conflict that give rise to particular behavioral dyadic interaction patterns observed in the last chapter and those that involve divorcing partners needing to be mediated by a third party. Whereas the sources of conflict in the last chapter are partners' problematic behaviors that turn out to be quite numerous, the latter are issues or social concerns and are more limited in number.

According to Deutsch (1973), theoretically, interdependent disputants engage in conflict over one or more of the following five types of issues:

Control over resources. Space, money, property, children, and so forth, which may be viewed as not sharable.

Preferences and nuisances. Activities of one person impinge on another's preferences, sensitivities, or sensibilities.

Values. Concerning what should be, including religious and ideological issues.

Beliefs. Concerning what is; what are the facts; reality.

The nature of the relationship. Repair and redefinition of personal and social relationships.

The typical conflict areas for divorcing couples appear to conform to Deutsch's general typology of dispute issues. Milne (1986) draws on experience as a mediator to identify the issues as essentially contractual and involving conflict over control of resources (finances including alimony, property division, child support, legal/physical custody, and visitation). Because the large number of divorces occurring in the United States today involve many children, they are of paramount concern. As reported by

Jones (1988), other legal issues may arise involving conflict over preferences/nuisances (moral fitness and appropriate actions of custodial parent such as sexual relationships and substance abuse), kidnapping one's children, or physical damage to one another's property. In addition, there are nonlegal issues regarding values and beliefs (philosophical differences in childrearing). Finally, there is conflict over the nature of the relationship (sexual relations; alleged actual or threatened physical harm).

When they engage in the divorcing process, the conflict between partners takes on a particular twist because of society's interest in the matter. Thus, many conflicts of interest are social issues as well. For example, in the eyes of society, ending a marital relationship does not end a parental relationship; therefore, divorce mediation often deals with child-related issues.

Moreover, although the conflicts appear to focus on one another's specific behaviors or values, they actually deal more with rules, norms, and roles. Mediation involves redefining the partners' relationship. The new relationship differs from the former one in that new rules, norms, and roles are negotiated with the help of a third party.

After reviewing the mediated cases at a university child psychiatric outpatient clinic, Veltkamp and Miller (1988) provide a classification scheme for compiling data on mediation. These categories concern conflicts over the rules, norms, and roles that must be negotiated to resolve disputes over the visitation plan, custodial plan, the presence of physical or sexual abuse by a parent, parental adequacy in general, and poor or unstable living conditions of a parent.

Triadic Conflict Behavioral Interaction Measures

Whereas the coding schemes in Chapter 2 involved a dyad in which paired interactions were behaviorally coded, the coding schemes in this chapter apply to a triad in which the divorcing partners and the mediator together are behaviorally coded. If this should appear to be a minor alteration in method, it should be pointed out that the addition of a third party changes the perspective that researchers must take when gathering data and theorizing about the conflict process.

Separate groups of researchers have devised different interventionist measures based essentially on overlapping data from the same resource (Donohue et al., 1988; Jones, 1988; Slaikeu, Culler, Pearson, & Thoennes, 1985). These data are derived from 80 audiotapes from three centers in Los Angeles, Hartford, and Minneapolis, collected by Jessica Pearson as part of the Divorce Mediation Research Project (1981–1984), funded by the Children's Bureau of the U.S. Department of Health and Human Services (90-CW-634).

Donohue's Interaction Coding Scheme

Donohue et al. (1988) coded spouse and mediator verbal acts using a scheme developed by Donohue (1981) originally devised for coding plaintiff–defendant interaction negotiation, based on the Rogers and Farace (1975) relational control scheme. Donohue proceeded, however, to make modifications that related more to biding and distinguished between cue and response codes. The cue and response functions of communication were separated such that each utterance was coded as a response to a prior utterance and a cue to a subsequent utterance. In addition, a more comprehensive set of cue codes relating especially to the negotiation process were included. Finally, the cue and response codes were designed to examine the dynamics of negotiation by focusing on the following tactics:

> *Attacking.* Personal accusations; negative evaluations.
> *Defending/bolstering.* Presenting proposals, providing information, requesting information or clarification, providing a rationale for one's position.
> *Regressing/integrating.* Any utterance that agreed with the prior utterance, demonstrated support for a proposal or position.

Thus, Donohue's scheme for coding divorce mediation preserves the competition–cooperation orientation. While the attack and defending codes capture the competitive communication acts, the regressing–integrating codes are used to identify the cooperative communication acts.

Donohue et al. (1988) add to Donohue's interaction analysis scheme the following categories to code the mediator's interventions:

> *Structuring.* Identifying and enforcing interaction rules designed to overcome "dysfunctional communication patterns."
>
> *Reframing.* Helping to restructure disputants' own proposals; pointing out areas of agreement.
>
> *Expanding/requesting.* Requesting proposals; requesting clarification of proposals; requesting reaction to proposals.

Unlike the next measure to be reviewed, Donohue's instrument may be used in other mediation contexts besides divorce (e.g., where neighbors, students–teachers, and college roommates attempt to mediate disputes).

The unit of analysis was the communication act defined as an uninterrupted talking turn. Coders were asked to focus on the utterance prior to and subsequent to the intervention to determine the role played by the mediator's communication acts in the spouses' attack, defend, and integrate communication acts. Reliability (or agreement) between coders ranged from .69 to .71 for the three categories of mediator interventions, and .78 to .80 for the disputant attack, bolster, and integration categories.

Slaikeu's Mediation Process Analysis

Slaikeu, Culler, et al. (1985) and Jones (1988) coded both spouse and mediator verbal and nonverbal (affect, tone) communication acts, using a scheme developed by Slaikeu, Pearson, Luckett, and Myers (1985) that resulted in the Mediation Process Analysis (MPA). The instrument consisted of the following eight content codes:

Process. Statements or questions regarding mediation issues; relevance of remarks, suggestions regarding mediation actions.

Information. Factual information about the mediation process and its alternatives, the children, and the spouses.

Summarize other. Restatements/rephrasing other's statements.

Self-disclosure. Statements indicating agreement or disagreement, expression of feelings, empathic statements.

Attributions. Statements attributing attitudes or actions to the spouses, children, and others.

Proposed solution. Solutions regarding either party or both; problems with the solution.

Agreements. Statements of agreements made before, during, and toward the end of mediation; statements regarding disputes that could arise in the future.

Interruptions. Including who was interrupted and who did the interrupting. (Only when a broken statement was not resumed was it coded as an interruption.)

Slaikeu and his colleagues also included the tone (affect) of the verbal statements. Therefore, in addition to the eight content codes, the MPA also required that the coders assign one of three following tone codes to each unit:

Positive. The tone of voice denotes warmth, cooperation, understanding, humor, encouragement, or enthusiasm.

Negative. Tone indicates irritation, lack of cooperativeness, anger, sarcasm, or threat.

Neutral. Tone conveys no obvious pleasure or displeasure.

Included in their discussion of this instrument, Slaikeu, Pearson et al. (1985) reported reliability or agreement between coders of .90 or better and provide a manual for coding the content and tone of the divorce mediation.

Unlike the one devised by Donohue, Slaikeu's coding scheme is not tied directly to a competition–cooperation dichotomy but more directly emphasizes the role of affect and is designed specifically for divorce mediation. Moreover, an attempt is made to capture a broader range of categories to give a more general description of the interaction patterns typical of divorce mediation. By applying both Donohue's and Slaikeu's coding schemes to data derived from the same resource, one might better understand the role of the mediator and how her or his actions help to settle disputes.

Some Communication Differences Between Settled and Unsettled Disputes

Only recently have systematic, objective, empirical approaches been applied to divorce mediation. Among these studies, few conform to the rules–interventionist paradigm. This approach employs a variety of measures including behavioral coding schemes and a triadic model that consists of the communication acts produced by both divorcing partners and the mediator. Rules–interventionist researchers assume that active participation by the interventionist alters the outcome of mediation, and a mediator who sets up rules and structures the mediation sessions is more likely to produce agreement between the parties.

Recently, the rules–interventionist approach has attempted to answer the question: What role does the mediator play in helping divorcing couples restore constructive communication for the resolution of issues? Before discussing the answer to that question, it is important to understand how mediation fits into the larger picture of the overall divorce process itself.

In the context of divorce, a couple separates into autonomous identities and moves through a series of stages in which the participants must deal with changing definitions of reality, both for themselves and for others (Vaughan, 1979). The marital dissolution process actually consists of six divorces or "stations" (Bohannan, 1970).

1. *Emotional divorce.* A time of deliberation and despair. One or both partners try to deny the phenomenon of divorce and hope the crisis will be averted.

2. *Legal divorce.* A time of legal involvement. Partners consult with an attorney and/or mediator.
3. *Economic divorce.* A time of loneliness and relief. Partners separate physically and arrange for alimony and division of property.
4. *Coparental divorce and problems of custody.* A time of concern for children. Divorcing partners work out an agreement for custody, maintenance, and visitation.
5. *Community divorce.* A time of excitement and regret. Ex-partners make new social contacts and undertake a new life-style.
6. *Psychic divorce.* A time of acceptance and independence. Ex-partners and children accept finality of divorce.

Crosby, Gage, and Raymond (1983) content-analyzed detailed essays by persons who provided accounts of their divorce experience. Although a progression through divorce stages did appear, it was concluded that the process was more complicated than a simple transition from one station to the next and often with one person lagging at least slightly behind the partner who actively pursued the divorce.

The observed stations of divorce and nonmutuality of the divorce decision suggest that mediation should be viewed as a complex process. Before observing interaction during the mediation sessions, it is important to understand who seeks mediation.

Antecedents: Who Seeks Mediation and Benefits from It?

While it is difficult to predict for a specific person or in a given case who might seek mediation and best succeed at it, there are patterns that emerge when examining a large number of cases. First, who seeks mediation rather than litigation?

Socioeconomic status. According to Pearson, Thoennes, and Vanderkooi (1982), mediation-prone parties tend to score higher on traditional socioeconomic indicators (e.g., income and education).

Favorable attitudes toward mediation/flexibility. Divorcing couples are more likely to choose mediation if they are prone to cooperation, are interested in reconciliation, and are more receptive to innovations and new technologies (Scanzoni & Polonko, 1980; Pearson et al., 1982).

Negative attitudes toward the court system. People who feel that the court system is less remote and impersonal or perceive their chances of winning better than in the court system prefer mediation (Pearson et al., 1982).

Attorneys' encouragement. Couples who are encouraged by their attorneys to try to resolve their differences through mediation are more likely to use mediation services (Pearson et al., 1982).

Gender. Men are slightly more interested than women in mediation (Pearson et al., 1982).

Who best succeeds by mediation? Due to the nature of a couple's relationship (Kressel et al., 1980) or the particular stage of divorce, mediation is not appropriate for all divorcing couples. Mediators need to recognize the situations that call for marital therapy, mediation, or litigation. According to Wallerstein (1986/1987), couples should seek mediation if they (1) are in need of a benign authority and guidance, (2) are fighting for child custody, and (3) remain "enmeshed" (unable to resolve conflicts by themselves due to nature of the relationship) but are able to separate the child's interests from their own. Other principles are as follows:

Equality of power. Veltkamp and Miller (1988) report that the success of mediation can only occur when both parties experience equal control and power in the process. Since abused wives are rarely treated equally by their husbands, they often find that they are better off in the court system which protects "weaker" parties (Lerman, 1984).

Favorable attitudes and instrumental skills. "[T]he parties' belief and acceptance of the (mediation) process shapes the prospects for success" (Kressel, 1987, p. 71). The ability to communicate and negotiate is an asset in divorce mediation

(Kressel et al., 1980; Pearson et al., 1982; Scanzoni & Polonko, 1980). Successful disputants act in a cooperative manner as indicated by their willingness to work together and share information, while unsuccessful parties act in a competitive way as indicated by their confrontations and lack of clearly defined patterns (Werner, 1990).

Intensity of the dispute. Lower levels of anger are associated with more successful mediation (Kochan & Jick, 1978; Kressel, 1987; Kressel et al., 1980). Veltkamp and Miller (1988) claim that many highly conflicted couples are more likely to choose the litigation process as a means of punishing the spouse.

Couple's history. The history of the relationship is also a factor. Divorcing spouses may have had a lengthy and problem-ridden history with deeply established patterns of action that are often uncooperative, abusive, noncommunicative, and domineering (Pearson & Thoennes, 1985). Kressel et al. (1980) have found that the nature of a couple's relationship is key in determining the success of mediation. They found that some types of relationships (for details, see Kressel et al., 1980) were not likely to produce rewarding results in mediation.

Couple's resources. "The less there is to divide, the less successful the mediator is likely to be" (Kressel, 1987, p. 71).

High motivation to reach settlement. Parties are more likely to settle if motivated, for example, by impending court-imposed settlement (Kressel, 1987).

The remainder of this chapter examines the role of the mediator, particularly his or her ability to facilitate communication between the divorcing pair. The mediator's influence is especially important when the parties are unfamiliar with the bargaining process. To better understand the role of the mediator, observational measures are useful.

Mediator Actions

In spite of the difficulty in gaining access to information as noted earlier, the mediation process has been studied to some extent using both self-reports of spouses' satisfaction with the outcomes and interaction coding schemes applied to audiotaped spouse mediation sessions including intervention by the mediator. By observing triadic patterns of interaction, researchers are able to identify mediator actions that produce more mutually satisfying agreements.

Donohue and His Colleagues' Research on Interventionist Communication Acts. Using the coding scheme devised by Donohue (1981), Donohue et al. (1988) found that successful mediators were more likely than unsuccessful ones to use more intense structuring and reframing interventions in response to attacks. The more successful mediators were also more likely to rephrase negative comments into more positive ones. Donohue and Weider-Hatfield (1988) coded 20 custody–visitation sessions (10 reaching agreement; 10 not reaching agreement). They found that more successful mediators were more in control of the mediation, used more interventions to involve the divorcing partners in finding the information necessary for agreement, and distributed more of these interventions fairly and consistently between disputants.

Slaikeu and His Colleagues' Research on Intervention Communication. To code mediator communication behavior and divorcing partners' interaction acts among couples who reached agreement on child custody and those who did not as a result of mediation, Slaikeu, Culler, et al. (1985) used the scheme created by Slaikeu, Pearson, et al. (1985). The most important difference between cases that settled successfully and those that did not was the amount of time mediators were expected to spend on discussing the terms to include in a final settlement. In the successful cases, mediators not only felt obligated to spend more time discussing these terms but also were expected to spend more time discussing possible solutions in general. They were not expected to spend much time explaining the mediation process to the spouses, requesting disclosures of feelings, and making attributions about the attitudes of the other parties.

In all the cases combined, the researchers discovered the following patterns of actions implying that other rules are also operating:

Speaker time was fairly evenly divided among three parties: the two spouses and the mediator.

Whereas mediators tended to address both spouses, husbands and wives generally directed their remarks to the mediator.

Mediators tended to be responsible for most of the questioning in a mediation session.

Mediators expressed statements on procedural issues three times more than did disputants. Mediators conveyed information on what mediation is (25% of utterances) and made statements regarding the process itself (13%).

Mediators tended to offer more statements summarizing the spouses' comments than did either party.

Spouses emitted more emotionally toned statements than did the mediator.

Mediators engaged in only about half as many attribution statements as did spouses. More than 35% of the statements made by both spouses were self-disclosures. Another 20% were attributions about the attitudes, motives, and actions of others, usually the other spouse.

Perhaps in an effort to establish rapport and encourage the spouses to share their feelings, mediators' statements showed more empathy than did the those uttered by the spouses.

Mediators attempted to balance proposals by specifying how both parties could be involved, while each spouse tended to specify what he or she could do.

Fewer than 3% of the statements were classified as interruptions (where the thought was not resumed).

Jones's Research on Phases of Mediation. According to Jones (1988), divorce mediation sessions that ended in agreement progressed from differentiation to integration through three phases (information exchange, problem solving, and finally resolution actions). Using a revised version of the MPA (Slaikeu, Pearson, et al., 1985),

Jones coded 18 agreement (where a formal written solution was completed) and 18 no-agreement divorce mediation sessions. Results revealed that no-agreement mediation never progressed beyond the first stage. It was characterized by a continuing emphasis on information exchange throughout mediation and by a deemphasis on problem solving and resolution actions. Jones obtained reliability or agreement between coders that ranged from .87 to .95 over the categories. Jones's findings could be interpreted within the rules–interventionist paradigm as additional evidence of cooperative rules defining and governing actions that facilitated agreement in successful or agreement mediation and competitive rules defining and governing actions that hindered it in unsuccessful or no-agreement mediation.

Jones also reported the following specific findings: First, in the successful sessions, mediators used significantly more process statements, summarization of other statements, and self-disclosure statements in the initial and middle segments of mediation than did mediators in nonagreement sessions. However, in much later segments, no-agreement mediators used more of these actions than did agreement mediators. Moreover, agreement mediators stated more solutions and agreements in middle and later segments than did no-agreement mediators. Again, the rules or expectations governing actions made in no-agreement mediation appear to differ from those that apply to agreement mediation.

The rules–interventionist approach has produced only a few empirical studies on couples' conflict. The approach has, however, generated many useful techniques for training mediators to successfully help couples develop agreements with which both partners can live.

STRUCTURED MEDIATION: HELPING DIVORCING SPOUSES SETTLE DISPUTES

In general, the rules–interventionist approach views conflicts of interest as mixed motive—a mixture of cooperative and competitive interests where a variety of outcomes is possible, such as mutual loss, gain for one and loss for the other, and mutual gain (Deutsch, 1973). It is notable that a distinguishing feature of these conflicts of interest is that both parties have something to gain from mediation (Reiches & Harral, 1974).

Because so much is at stake and trade-offs are expected, spouses may resort to a wide variety of tactics including concealing minimum dispositions (Putnam & Jones, 1982) and revealing more desirable positions (Reiches & Harral, 1974). The ability of each party and the mediator to form estimates of each partner's preferred position and his or her own minimum position is required since every proposal and counterproposal reflects the position strength of both parties (Beisecker, 1970). While an estimate of the other's position may be obtained prior to or during mediation through communication, as Druckman (1977) observes, the parties use rhetoric to cajole, mislead, persuade, and confirm one's opposite in a direction that could enhance one's own position. Thus, mediators must be aware of the tactics typically used by individuals in divorce mediation.

In addition to an awareness of persuasive techniques used by divorcing partners, mediators are trained to facilitate progress through seven stages (Taylor, 1988).

1. Creating structure and a climate of trust
2. Finding facts and isolating issues
3. Creating options and alternatives
4. Getting the parties involved in the decision-making process by getting them to negotiate their differences
5. Writing a plan based on agreements by parties
6. Having the plan reviewed by legal authorities and initiating legal processing
7. Reviewing, revising, and implementing the plan

According to Kressel (1987), as they guide mediation through the above stages, interventionists are expected to do the following: establish rapport with spouses, improve the negotiating climate, and be assertive (i.e., be highly active and directive). By gaining control of the interaction between spouses to build a structure that is productive for creating cooperation, mediators create and enforce rules in the form of structured interventions.

First, it is necessary to create rules that define the situation as cooperative in order to produce more cooperative action and to help the parties to understand how to integrate their own and the other's messages into a final agreement that satisfies both parties and their concerns. To do this the competent mediator functions as a translator who relabels and redefines concepts or creates new ones in an attempt to create a common language for mediating disputes. Mediators need to help the parties redefine themselves and their relationship which will necessitate that they relate to one another in new ways. To do this, mediators should define the roles of all participants in the mediation session. Moreover, redefining may be accomplished through reframing intervention which attempts to revise or create spouses' understanding of their relationship. By rewording emotionally laden statements, by stating negative comments in a more positive manner, and by explaining the value of a proposal, the mediator uses language effectively to provide an insight that can facilitate cooperative outcomes (Thoennes & Pearson, 1985). Mediators should explain the positive and negative consequences of various proposals, restate comments as proposals, identify areas of agreement, and offer their own proposals to stimulate discussion and consensus.

Next, according to Jones (1988), divorce mediators should discourage competitive behavior where disputants present their positions and attack the other's position and encourage cooperative behavior where they discuss mutual interests, goals, or desires. Several mediation programs structure the mediation process around a series of steps in which a cooperative, trusting atmosphere is created to promote collaboration between the parties (Saposnek, 1983; Folberg & Taylor, 1984; Moore, 1986). First, mediators are encouraged to enforce discussion rules regarding taking turns, interruptions, who speaks first, and who talks to whom. They should make it clear that they have the right to keep the discussion on track and to intervene when necessary.

Second, because of the adversarial relationship between the parties initially and the need for the mediator to establish credibility with them, Coogler (1978) argues that the mediator must work to create trust by laying down a few ground rules. One of these rules is to put the adversarial process, including attorneys, on hold. This rule helps create trust by eliminating the worry about being taken to court. Another ground rule is to fully and accurately disclose information regarding children, property, finances, and the parties' needs. To ensure confidentiality, the parties must agree not to call the mediator to testify in court or to introduce in court information obtained during settlement negotiations (Grebe, 1988). Specific rules and the rules approach in general are discussed in Coogler (1978) and Grebe (1988).

Because of the expectations associated with the role of mediator, interventionists benefit from training in the following skills:

Mediators are trained to employ a supportive and optimistic mode to lessen the chance that anxiety, anger, fear, and guilt will prevent resolution of the disputes (Petrossi, 1987).

Mediators are trained to employ creative interventions, humor, praising strengths, and building gradually to help the parties regain self-respect and develop flexibility (Hahn, 1987).

Mediators are trained to promote cooperation, communication, and problem solving rather than to advocate a particular position (Girdner, 1985). The mediator as a neutral, objective third party can only help the parties derive their own agreement (Kiely & Crary, 1986).

Mediators may be trained to analyze the situation (nature of the dispute and parties involved) and to choose the appropriate intervention approach from among several options (for details, see Potapchuk & Carlson, 1987).

Mediators are trained to sequence tasks from beginning to end of mediation including (1) meetings with both disputants to prepare them for mediation, (2) mediation sessions, (3) administration of background information forms, and (4) the

designing of a parental responsibilities agreement
(Marthaler, 1989). Details for accomplishing these tasks are
provided by Moore (1986).

Mediators may be trained to orient the divorcing couple to the
"Marital Mediation Rules" developed by the Family Mediation Association (Coogler et al., 1979).

Mediators need to foster understanding and empathy. Slaikeu,
Culler, et al. (1985) argue that understanding the other
party's view is important in successful divorce mediation. If
a couple lacks this ability, the mediator needs to foster it
perhaps by using the bilateral focus technique of Rapoport
(1964) which is more advanced than the active listening
technique described by Gordon (1970) and recommended by
Fisher and Ury (1981).

In addition, to the above skills, mediators need a thorough
understanding of mediator goals and tactics. According to Donohue
et al. (1985), interventionist goals and tactics useful in divorce
mediation include:

Structuring the process of mediation. This objective is met when
the mediator gains control of the mediation. Donohue et al.
(1985) detail five tactics that mediators may use to achieve
this goal: identifying or enforcing the interaction rules;
terminating or initiating discussion; identifying or enforcing
the agenda or topic; identifying the role and the process of
mediation; and providing orientation information about the
situation, mediation, or counseling.

Reframing the disputants' positions. This goal is achieved when
the parties take the information given and restructure it in a
more usable form, perhaps resulting in the creation of an
integrative agreement. Again, Donohue et al. (1985) list
several tactics that mediators may use to achieve this
objective: creating alternative proposals; negatively evaluating the disputant's proposal or position; reframing proposals
or reframing the utterances as a proposal; identifying and

reinforcing points of agreement and support for the utterance;
and providing a listening response to signal attentiveness.

Expanding the information resource. This objective is realized
when more information is provided to the parties and
mediator. Requesting tactics are also available (Donohue et
al., 1985): requesting an opinion or evaluation of the other's
proposal or opinion; requesting proposals; requesting clarification of a proposal or topic situation; requesting relational
or feeling information; and requesting clarification of a prior
utterance.

Thus, techniques exist for improving mediator competence to
achieve more successful mediation outcomes.

CONCLUSION

Rules–interventionists have explained how rules define and govern
successful mediation and have tied together mediator goals,
communication acts, and mediation outcomes. In theory, the
mediator restores communication and helps partners redefine their
relationship including their roles and responsibilities.

Researchers have developed schemes in which the mediator's
utterances are coded once as a response to a prior utterance by
either partner and once as a cue to the subsequent utterance.

However, divorce mediation is in need of a great deal more
empirical research. While there are a number of humanistic and
deductive essays on the topic, there are only a few empirical studies
on the role of the interventionist in divorce mediation. One reason
for this may be that the topic is "newer" as a research focus than the
study of conflict among spouses engaged in problem solving. In
addition, it should be pointed out that it is difficult to gain access to
real divorce mediation sessions because of the need to preserve
confidentiality that is often mandated by state laws. In the future,
trends and insights may be gained by more empirical research on
divorce mediation.

The coding of communication acts during divorce mediation reveals several differences in the rules defining and governing actions of mediators and spouses in cases where agreement is reached through mediation and in those which are not settled successfully (no-agreement).

While at least two measures have been adapted to divorce mediation, perhaps efforts could be directed toward creating a measure out of the process of divorce mediation itself. Donohue and his colleagues have developed a measure originally designed for coding plaintiff–defendant interaction negotiation, based on the Rogers and Farace relational control scheme. Moreover, the theoretical importance of relational control (competition–cooperation dichotomy) and of affect (tone of voice) may require that a single coding scheme contain the means for measuring both.

The rules–interventionist approach includes a mediator's communication acts when observing and recording a couple's behavioral interaction during divorce mediation. The focus is on triadic conflict communication patterns that lead to successful/agreement or unsuccessful/no-agreement outcomes. Although the role of the mediator has been of great interest since the inception of mediation, it is only recently that the rules–interventionist paradigm has emerged as one of the more preferred research approaches for the empirical study of divorce mediation. While it may meet some standards for a credible research paradigm, the rules–interventionist approach presently accounts for only a small number of empirical studies in divorce mediation. Moreover, many of these studies had access to the same limited pool of tapes for data analysis. Perhaps, in time and with access to a greater number of taped sessions from a larger geographical area, the rules–interventionist approach may become as popular a research paradigm as the cognitive–exchange approach examined in the next chapter.

FOUR

THE COGNITIVE–EXCHANGE PERSPECTIVE ON CONFLICT IN DEVELOPING INTIMATE RELATIONSHIPS

When thinking about the topic of conflict in intimate relationships, one probably envisions a couple engaged in a verbal disagreement. Thus, the systems–interactionist and rules–interventionist approaches seem obvious candidates for studying partners in conflict because they focus on communication patterns that occur during disagreements between partners. Moreover, the process nature of conflict is readily apparent in these two research perspectives because observers can actually see and hear the changes taking place during the interaction.

Cognitive–exchange researchers take an entirely different view of conflict as cognitive constructs, namely, strategies involving self and other perceptions and intentions that range from direct confrontation to avoidance. Since these cognitions are internal psychological constructs, the process nature of conflict is not as easily discernible to outside observers as it is when behaviors are observed within the other research paradigms. To "observe" conflict, others must ask partners to report their internal states or cognitions.

Because some strategies for managing conflict involve avoiding it all together, conflict may exist even when partners are not engaging in overt disagreement. From the cognitive–exchange perspective, to view conflict as a process means that one must use partners' reports of perceived sources of conflict that result in the selection of conflict management strategies which in turn influence the development of intimacy.

After a discussion of the basic concepts and theories that characterize the cognitive–exchange approach, this chapter reviews research that relates to the dominant paradigm and describes how intimate partners may be trained within this approach to manage their conflicts. Finally, the chapter concludes with an evaluation of the cognitive–exchange approach as a research paradigm.

BACKGROUND

Those who work within the cognitive–exchange paradigm have identified at least two important characteristics of intimate relationship development: satisfaction (positive affect or attraction to the relationships) and commitment (the tendency to maintain the relationship and to feel psychologically "attached" to it). A key idea behind the cognitive–exchange approach is that partners engage in social exchange in ways that lead to either relationship satisfaction and commitment or dissatisfaction and lack of commitment.

Social Exchange Theory

One of the distinguishing features of the paradigm is the notion of social exchange—in which human behaviors are viewed in terms of their utility and are associated with rewards and costs (e.g., Blau, 1964; Emerson, 1976, 1981; Homans, 1961; Kelley & Thibaut, 1978; Levi-Strauss, 1969; Thibaut & Kelley, 1959).

Rewards and Costs

People engage in behaviors that have consequences for others, and different behaviors have different consequences or outcomes. Although the value of behaviors is not universal, positive consequences such as pleasure and gratifications are usually seen as rewards and negative outcomes such as undesirable effort and social embarrassment are likely to be interpreted as costs. According to Homans (1961), people try to maximize profits and minimize costs, although they may forego short-term profits for long-term gains.

As depicted by Thibaut and Kelley (1959), individuals determine the value of a relationship by comparing it to a *personal point of reference or subjectively established comparison level* (CL). One's CL is a (minimal) baseline of rewards, relative to costs, of which she or he feels deserving. CL may also be considered a measure of one's attraction to a relationship. A satisfying or attractive relationship is derived from a reward–cost ratio that exceeds one's expectations, minimum, or neutral point. For example, in the conduct of her research within the cognitive–exchange paradigm, Rusbult (1983) uses one general item each to more specifically measure perceived rewards and costs of the primary relationship ("Initially, how rewarding was the relationship?" 1 = not at all, 9 = extremely rewarding; and "Initially how costly was the relationship?" 1 = not at all, 9 = extremely costly).

In addition to a CL based on perceived rewards and costs, relationship development is influenced by other social exchange variables, namely, perceived alternative attractions, perceived investments in the relationship, and perceived social pressure from others who comprise a social network in which partners are embedded.

Alternative Attractions

Social exchange theorists point out that in addition to CL, individuals also use *a comparison level for available alternative opportunities* (CL-alt) to help define the lowest level of outcomes a partner accepts from the primary relationship. This means that available alternatives (other people outside the primary relationship) appear more desirable when one sees that they offer better reward–cost ratios than he or she perceives in the primary relationship. In this case, CL-alt raises CL, although it could lower CL if the alternatives have less to offer than one's partner. Thus, CL-alt is a measure of one's dependence on or commitment to a relationship.

To better understand the concept of CL-alt, it is helpful to see how one researcher, Rusbult (1983), assesses the rewards and costs of alternative relationships in research. She asked respondents two questions: "[H]ow appealing are the people you could have dated other than your partner?" (1 = not at all; 9 = extremely appealing) and "To what extent can you be happy when you're not dating anyone?" (1 = not at all; 9 = extremely happy).

By combining Cl-alt with CL, one begins to better understand how long-term intimate relationships develop or deteriorate. Presumably, a rewarding relationship will continue, while a costly one deteriorates in time. Studies are usually conducted on newly formed and developing romantic relationships within the cognitive–exchange paradigm, but the approach may also help explain the dissolution of intimate relationships. If the costs of a long-term relationship begin to outweigh the rewards, the partners may pay close attention to the reward–cost ratio and perhaps explore alternative possibilities (Levinger, 1979). If, for example, some spouses who enter the workplace after several years of marriage develop satisfying lives outside the home, their comparison level for alternatives (CL-alt) rises and concurrently their expectations of what they should be receiving from their marriage (CL) also rise. For some, the inequities in their marital roles are more likely than before to be perceived and to become sources of friction at home (Scanzoni, 1979a). They may seek divorce when the expected net benefits of their marriage compare unfavorably to the perceived alternatives. More details on social exchange theory and its application to family research are provided by Nye (1979).

Some scholars argue that the notion of social exchange applies only to newly forming relationships or later formed relationships that are now in serious trouble and is less relevant to mature and continuing relationships. Perhaps, partners in satisfactory long-term associations who have "an economy of surplus" can imagine countless instances in which they have received benefits or are likely to receive more, making them less likely to keep count (Levinger, 1979). Thus, partners are more likely to attend to the exchange ratios during the formative and declining stages than when relating mutually during a stable middle stage.

It is difficult, however, to imagine that mature and continuing relationships are so free of problems that partners do not need to reassess their relationship and alternative attractions. Like partners in newly forming relationships, and those in developed ones now dissolving, partners in mature, continuing relationships may experience moments when they mentally compare perceptions of one another's rewards and costs with perceptions of those offered by alternative attractions.

In addition to rewards and costs, cognitive–exchange researchers have shown that the size of investments in the relationship and social pressure from others affect the extent to which CL and CL-alt influence relationship satisfaction and commitment.

Investment Theory

Investment theory (Rusbult, 1980) suggests that increasing interdependence makes termination of an intimate relationship potentially more costly. The theory predicts that persons experience greater satisfaction with a relationship if they have invested sizable or numerous resources in that involvement.

Rusbult has clarified the concept of investment in relationships by developing general and concrete self-reports to measure it. The general measures of initial investment size asked respondents the following questions: "Initially how much had you invested in the relationship?" (1 = very little; 9 = very much invested) and "At what point would you have lost by ending the relationship?" (1 = lost a great deal; 9 = lost nothing). The concrete items asked respondents to rate the number of mutual friends, duration of acquaintance, hours per week spent together, extent of shared "memories" or events, extent of monetary investments, number of shared possessions, number of activities uniquely associated with the relationship, size of emotional investment, and extent of self-disclosure.

To show how investment operates with several other social exchange variables to affect relationship commitment, Rusbult (1983) gave respondents (17 male and 17 female undergraduate, dating couples) an initial questionnaire and a set of 12 relationship questionnaires designed to measure perceived rewards, costs, alternatives, investments in the relationship, relationship satisfaction, and commitment. Rusbult found that increases in reward over time led to corresponding increases in satisfaction and commitment. Because of increases in satisfaction, declines in the quality of available alternatives, and increases in investment size, commitment increased. Rusbult also found evidence of "entrapment"— relatively low levels of satisfaction accompanied by a decline in quality of alternatives but heavy investment in the relationship. Evidence pointed to the importance of changes over time in commitment due to increasing investments.

As a test of the generalizability of the investment theory, Rusbult, Johnson, and Morrow (1986a) recruited by sampling from a telephone directory 130 individuals who were currently involved in serious relationships. They were administered a set of questionnaires developed by Rusbult (1983). Consistent with investment model predictions, an increase in rewards was associated with an increase in satisfaction and commitment. Again, decreases in quality of alternatives and increases in investment were associated with increases in commitment.

There appear to be male–female differences in the role of investments in some relationships. In courtship, for example, some cognitive–exchange researchers argue that compared to men, women are more cautiously pragmatic during early encounters because they potentially have more to lose. It has been shown that, in heterosexual relationships, men report falling in love more quickly than do women (Levinger, 1979), and that women are more discriminating than men in mate selection, are slower than men to fall in love, and supposedly lose more than men by staying in love too long with the wrong person (Hill, Rubin, & Peplau, 1976).

Perceived Pressures from Friends, Relatives, and Others

In addition to reporting their judgments regarding rewards, costs, alternative attractions, investments, and other cognitive variables, researchers may ask partners to evaluate the perceived influence of other members of their social network (e.g., friends and relatives). Levinger (1979), Green and Sporakowski (1983), and Milardo (1983) examine romantic and married dyads within couples' social contacts. Perceived social influence is viewed as a source of either relationship support or discouragement as an individual makes decisions about rewards and costs provided by a partner and alternative attractions.

Parks, Stan, and Eggert (1983) describe a self-report that measures the influence of a social network on a couple's romantic involvement. After Parks and his colleagues asked respondents to identify those people who make up a couple's social network, they asked them to report the amount of support they perceived from each person by indicating how much they agreed with each of the following statements: "This person does not (or would not) approve of my current dating relationship" and "This person has often expressed approval or support for my current dating relationship." Responses were recorded on scales ranging in rating from one to five.

Americans do consult and take into consideration the opinions of friends, relatives, colleagues at work, and other members of their social networks (Cahn, 1987). Formal evidence for this social influence may be found in a variety of studies. Burr (1973) demonstrates that approval provided by key individuals where one works is associated with marital adjustment. Lewis (1973) shows that support from one's own family and friends is positively related to several relationship formation indices and negatively related to premarital disengagements. Krain (1977) finds that support from family and friends is associated with courtship progression. Parks et al. (1983) observe that romantic involvement is positively associated with perceived support from one's own and the partner's network of family and friends. This perceived support is influenced by attraction to network members, communication with them, and the number of people met in the networks.

The existence of an informal social network helps explain why some individuals choose to stay in a dissatisfying relationship even if there is a more desirable alternative. Out of a sense of duty and feelings of obligation, one may feel constrained from putting oneself first. Moreover, given a particular degree of dissatisfaction, a change in social pressure may provide an opportunity for disengagement. A friendship, love affair, or marriage could break up after the elimination of certain external pressures that helped to keep the relationship together physically. Thus, changes in the network of friends, relatives, and other important persons may have implications for commitment to an intimate relationship.

How Social Exchange Theory Fits into the Study of Conflict

Conflict and Relationship Satisfaction

Regarding courtship, Braiker and Kelley (1979) argue that CL viewed as relationship satisfaction depends on the following four factors:

> Love: caring, needing, and attachment;
> Conflict/negativity: conflict, arguments, problems;
> Ambivalence: confusion about feelings toward the partner; and
> Maintenance behavior: problem solving.

According to Braiker and Kelley, these dimensions of relationship satisfaction reflect "both the nature of the interdependence and the kinds of conflicts occurring in the relationship's course" (pp. 147–148). The degree of interdependence is reflected in the love category by references to caring, needing, and attachment (e.g., doing things for each other, spending time together, acting like a couple). The conflict/negative affect category indicates interpersonal conflict (arguments, disagreements), and the ambivalence category reflects internal conflict within the individual (e.g., confusion about partners' feelings toward one another). The maintenance category is represented by references to self-disclosure, efforts to change, and efforts to solve problems (e.g., spending time trying to work out problems, telling partner what each needs or wants from the relationship). It would seem that ambivalence, conflict/negativity, inability to solve problems and talk things out, and lack of love would lead to relationship dissatisfaction and lack of commitment.

Perception/Attribution/Efficacy Theory

The cognitive–exchange approach takes the position that the value of rewards and costs are in the "eye of the beholder." This calls attention to male–female differences that affect partners' perceptions of rewards and costs and their role in conflict. Men appear to differ from women in the way they perceive conflict, which in turn affects their relationship satisfaction. Lloyd (1987, 1990) has asked dating partners to keep daily observation records of conflicts over a 2-week period. She has found that the perception that there are many unresolved conflicts is most salient to women's perceived relationship satisfaction, whereas the perception of a large number and the stability of conflicts (i.e., the same issues coming up again and again) are most salient to men's relationship satisfaction.

Other male–female differences in perceptual processes have been found to have an impact on conflict in intimate relationships by distorting the intent of the message sent by one partner and the impact of that message on the other partner. Because of the strong behavioral influence on systems–interactionists (see Chapter 2), they tend to avoid the study of more abstract or subjective variables (e.g., perception and intent) that cannot be observed directly in couples' interaction. However, as reported in Chapter 1, sometimes researchers make contributions to more than one paradigm. This is a case in point where a few researchers who normally work within the systems–interactionist paradigm have found that while dissatisfied spouses may not differ with respect to their intentions, they may perceive their partner's remarks differently. For example, Gottman, whose contributions to the systems–interactionist paradigm were discussed in Chapter 2, and his colleagues report that the behavior of the dissatisfied spouses compared to satisfied spouses is perceived more negatively by partners than intended (Gottman, Notarius, Gonso, et al., 1976). This confirms an earlier finding that dissatisfied husbands are more inclined than those who are satisfied to attribute "negative connotations" to their wives' attempts to communicate affection, happiness, and playfulness (Kahn, 1970).

Male–female differences in perception are not the only internal processes that influences conflict in intimate relationships. Attribution processes help explain and predict the development of intimacy (Heider, 1958; Kelley, 1971) and outcomes of conflict messages (Canary & Spitzberg, 1989, 1990). For example, Fincham, Bradbury, and Grych (1990) argue that attributions of blame or intent give rise to hostile behavior such as retaliation.

> Retaliation is most likely when the partner is seen to have violated deliberately a central relationship rule for which no extenuating circumstances can be found; the partner is most likely to be seen as behaving with malevolent intent or selfish motivation. Such a situation will generate the most intense anger and may lead the perceiver to view retaliation as the partner's "just deserts." (p. 174)

According to Sillars (1980a), the simple choice of confronting or avoiding a conflict hinges on attributions like those revealed by the following questions: Were the abrasive actions of the partner intentional or not (causal judgment)? Is the person "reasonable" and approachable about the conflict (social inferences)? Is the person likely to continue with similar actions in the future (predicted outcomes)? Thus, sources of conflict and the strategy partners adopt for coping with the conflict are influenced by their attributions for the conflict.

In addition to attribution processes, Fincham et al. (1990) call attention to "efficacy expectations," which represent the individual's "belief that constructive problem-solving behavior can be executed" (pp. 171–172). Regardless of one's attributions of cause, responsibility, and blame, given low efficacy expectations, a partner is unlikely to engage in efforts to resolve the conflict and will choose to avoid it or withdraw from it. Given high efficacy expectations, however, the person is likely to undertake such efforts and confront the problem. In such cases, resolution attempts are directed toward that which is perceived as most easily changed and likely to produce satisfactory results (Fincham & Bradbury, 1987a). Efficacy expectations, along with commitment to the relationship and negative affect regarding the partner, influence predictions of conflict behavior.

CONFLICT AND RELATIONSHIP DEVELOPMENT: SUPPORTING RESEARCH WITHIN A COGNITIVE–EXCHANGE APPROACH

The discovery or identification of cognitive variables within the cognitive–exchange approach is made difficult by the fact that the data (e.g., cognition) are not readily observable to others as overt behaviors are. Because the data are often subjective and consist of general impressions formed by partners after observing a wide variety of their interactions over several months or years, researchers incorporate self-report instruments. For this reason, a word should be said about this form of measurement.

Strictly speaking, the cognitive–exchange approach is not synonymous with self-report questionnaires. Advocates of other research paradigms use them, and some cognitive–exchange researchers may gather objective behavioral data. However, with but few exceptions, the cognitive–exchange approach to the study of conflict between intimates relies heavily on self-report questionnaires of a type first pioneered by sociologists. In studies of conflicts between intimates using a questionnaire approach, intimate partners are typically asked to make inferences or attributions, to record or recall feelings, attitudes, and perceived behaviors, or to state what they intend to do (strategies). Respondents use these measures to report perceived sources of conflict and their cognitive responses to them.

Perceived Sources of Conflict?

The cognitive–exchange approach sees the sources of conflict as a self-reported perceived imbalance in resources of social exchange, love/sex/affection, perceived inequity, unequal power, or a general concept of relationship dissatisfaction. Although highly interrelated, each of these sources of conflict is discussed separately below.

Perceived Imbalance in Resources of Social Exchange

Hill et al. (1976), published a study of romantic pairs who were undergraduates at four colleges in the Boston area. Initially, these researchers mailed self-report types of questionnaires to a random sample of couples. A follow-up questionnaire was administered in person or by mail 6 months, 1 year, and 2 years after the initial self-reports were completed. By the end of the 2-year study period, 103 couples had broken up. The researchers found that perceived unequal involvement in the relationship (as suggested by social exchange theory), as well as other perceptions regarding discrepant age, educational aspirations, intelligence, and physical attractiveness, were among the reasons most often given for breaking up. A male–female difference was also found: Women were more likely than men to perceive discrepancies in their relationship involvement and somewhat more likely to be the ones to precipitate the breakups.

Building on a system that Foa and Foa (1974) originally devised and based on a review of the research literature, Rettig and Bubolz (1983) hypothesized that marital satisfaction depends on feelings about seven resources available for exchange in the following order of importance: (1) love (nonverbal expressions of positive regard, warmth, or comfort), (2) status (verbal expressions of high or low prestige or esteem), (3) service (labor of one for another), (4) information (advice, opinions, instructions, or enlightenment), (5) goods (contributions of material goods), (6) money (financial contributions), and (7) shared time (time spent together). Obtaining data by survey using self-administered questionnaires from 224 married couples, Rettig and Bubolz observed that husbands and wives experienced marriage differently. Husbands tended to value more highly the instrumental dimension of the relationship (e.g., cooked meals, household repairs), while wives emphasized the affectional dimension of the relationship (e.g., acceptance, affection, and approval). The authors concluded that the best kind of marriage seemed to be one in which partners felt that they got what they deserved.

Love/Sex/Affection

Differences in male–female perspectives have received additional attention on the first and most important of the resources of exchange, love/sex/affection. As Scanzoni (1979a) indicates, variations in conflict management strategies may be taken to represent the interests, goals, or rewards that men tend to associate with love (e.g., sexual gratification) that differ from those that women often associate with love (e.g., emotional intimacy, security). According to Nye (1979), a preponderance of studies report that men and women experience love and sex differently. These studies suggest that the following differences may function as sources of conflict:

> The possibility of an unwanted pregnancy is perceived to be more costly by women than by men.
> Societal sanctions against sexual intercourse are stronger for women than for men.
> Feelings of tension and frustration from incomplete sexual experiences are more frequent for women than for men.
> Women are more likely than men to prefer marriage as a precondition for sexual intercourse.
> Married men are more likely to engage in extramarital sexual intercourse than are married women.

More recent research continues to support male–female differences in perspectives on love/sex/affection. Buss (1989) conducted a series of tests that involved comparing 600 men's and women's self-reported judgments about the magnitude of the upset elicited by each of 15 major classes of conflict. Initially Buss asked 107 undergraduate men and women to list and describe in detail four acts or behaviors that intimates do that upset, irritate, hurt, or anger the opposite sex. Content analysis of these judgments revealed 147 distinct sources of conflict. Two versions of the same instrument, one for men and one for women, were created in which each sex was asked to rate each of these sources starting with "She . . ." on the men's version and "He . . ." on the women's. Factor analysis revealed that the 147 complaints fell into 15 specific groups. Buss then conducted a second set of tests that involved comparing men and women's judgments about the magnitude of the upset elicited by each of the major classes of conflict. Results from these judgments revealed that women were far more upset than were men by perceptions of their partner's sexual aggressiveness, whereas men were more upset than women by perceptions of their partner's sexual withholding. The data were explained in terms of the different reproductive interests typical of the two sexes. Arguing that the male investment tended to be smaller than the female investment in sex and that males did not incur the direct "costs" associated with pregnancy as did females, males appeared more indiscriminate, sexually aggressive, and "wanton." Whenever the interests of intimate men and women failed to coincide, Buss noted that there was potential for conflict.

Perceived Inequity

Equity theory (Hatfield, Utne, & Traupmann, 1979; Walster, Walster, & Berscheid, 1978) predicts that when individuals perceive themselves to be in inequitable relationships, they become distressed, which will motivate them to restore equity (Hatfield et al., 1979). Conversely, equity theory predicts that men and women in equitable relationships are more content than those in relationships where there is inequity. Utne, Hatfield, Traupmann, and Greenberger (1984) discuss measures of perceived equity, including the Walster Global Measure of Equity/Inequity and the finer-grained Traupman-Utne-Walster (TUW) scale. The global measure is designed to assess men's and women's general impressions about the perceived fairness of resource exchange that characterizes their relationships. The TUW scale focuses on four different areas:

> *Personal concerns.* How attractive spouses are, how sociable, and how intelligent.
>
> *Emotional concerns.* How much spouses like and love each other, understand each other, sex, commitment.
>
> *Day-to-day concerns.* How much money both bring in, house maintenance, being easy to live with, fitting in socially.
>
> *Opportunities gained or lost.* Opportunity to be married or married to someone else, to have children.

On the basis of their scores on the global and more specific measures, men and women are classified into three groups:

> *The "overbenefited."* Those men and women who are receiving more than they feel they deserve from their marriages.
>
> *The equitably treated.* Those who are receiving just what they think they deserve from their marriages.
>
> *The "underbenefited."* Those who are receiving less than they feel they deserve from their marriages.

Shown to be predictive in casual encounters, later equity theory was extended by Utne et al. (1984) to marital satisfaction and stability. Husbands and wives of 118 newly married couples, ages 16–45, in Madison, Wisconsin, were interviewed separately. Measures of marital equity, marital contentment/distress, and marital stability were taken. As predicted, results showed that spouses who felt equitably treated were more content in their marriage and perceived the marriage as more stable than did men and women in inequitable marriages. Neither women nor men appeared to be differentially concerned with equity.

Moreover, Sabatelli and Cecil-Pigo (1985) examined the relationship between interdependence—characterized by satisfaction, perceived equity, and the development of internal and external barriers to the dissolution of relationships—and commitment in intimate dyads. Using a cognitive–exchange perspective, Sabatelli and Cecil-Pigo hypothesized that commitment to a relationship should be accompanied by feelings of interdependence. Three hundred and one married persons residing in Dane County, Wisconsin, were randomly selected to complete a marital comparison level index (satisfaction), a relational equity scale (equity), a "barriers to marital dissolution" scale (barriers), and a relational commitment scale (commitment). Results supported the hypothesis in that the three indicators of interdependence increased along with increases in commitment. Of the three indicators of interdependence, perceived equity in the distribution of outcomes within a relationship was the variable found to account most for commitment for both husbands and wives.

Perceived Unequal Distribution of Power

Perceived unequal distribution of power in a relationship often results in conflict between intimates. In unequal relationships, one partner dominates the other. However, dissatisfied couples report that their partners are more coercive and less cognitive in their conflict discussions (Billings, 1979). Research findings show that husband dominance is a common problem because many wives indicate that they would prefer less controlling behavior from their husbands (Hawkins et al., 1980). According to a detailed study by Ting-Toomey (1984), couples who share power equally rank highest in marital satisfaction, husband-dominant couples rank medium, and wife-dominant couples rank lowest in marital satisfaction.

Relationship Dissatisfaction as a Source of Conflict

As argued earlier, conflict/negativity may lead to relationship dissatisfaction; however, relationship dissatisfaction may, itself, be perceived as a source of conflict. Perceived imbalance in the resources of exchange, inequity, and unequal distribution of power in a relationship appear to be quite specific when compared to a more general notion of relationship dissatisfaction. When studying relationship dissatisfaction in general as a source of conflict, either researchers use self-report techniques to assess the degree of dissatisfaction in the relationship or they use techniques to induce or manipulate partners' dissatisfaction with their relationship.

In addition to viewing subjectively reported relationship dissatisfaction as a source of conflict, cognitive–exchange researchers use the relationship dissatisfaction concept in a way that differs from other researchers (e.g., systems–interactionists). In this approach, cognitive variables like relationship dissatisfaction are believed to be capable of producing behavioral and cognitive effects. Thus, relationship dissatisfaction may influence one's preference for particular confrontation and conflict avoidance strategies.

To measure general dissatisfaction with a romantic relationship, Rusbult (1983) devised three subscales:

How much do you like your partner? (1 = I like him/her very much; 9 = not at all)

To what extent are you attracted to your partner? (1 = not at all; 9 = extremely attracted to him/her)

To what degree are you satisfied with your relationship? (1 = extremely satisfied; 9 = not at all).

In other studies the concept of relationship dissatisfaction was manipulated. In one study, Rusbult, Zembrodt, and Gunn (1982) described to a respondent a partner who was low or high in attractiveness, in attraction to the respondent, and in relationship satisfaction and asked the respondent how she or he would evaluate a relationship with this person. In another study, Rusbult and Zembrodt (1983) asked undergraduate students to write an essay in response to a time in their lives when they became dissatisfied with a romantic relationship in which they were involved. Finally,

Rusbult, Johnson, and Morrow (1986b) asked respondents to think of a situation when they were unhappy with their partner, where the partner said/did things the respondents did not like, when the respondents had problems in their relationship, or when they were upset by their partner. Thus, Rusbult used techniques for inducing or manipulating general dissatisfaction with romantic relationships.

Conflict Management Typologies

Some researchers maintain that a focus on multiple responses is necessary to develop a theoretical typology sufficient to describe the full range of possible reactions to conflict situations. In the absence of such typologies, it is difficult to develop a comprehensive theory-based understanding of conflict between intimates. In the following discussion, alternative cognitive responses to conflict and conflict modes/styles are shown to be two different typologies of conflict management strategies.

Alternative Cognitive Responses (to Perceived Sources of Conflict)

There appear to be many strategies that could guide behavioral responses to sources of conflicts, and although one may prefer direct confrontation, there are in fact other strategies for managing conflicts in an intimate relationship. A few authors have deductively generated typologies of responses to conflict situations from theories of marital processes. For example, Chafetz (1980) has identified four conflict resolution strategies that spouses may use when attempting to alter their partner's behaviors: authority, control, influence, and manipulation. Cushman and I (Cushman & Cahn, 1985) have described four theoretical responses to relationship dissatisfaction as a source of conflicts: continuation, repair, renegotiation, and disengagement. Although a deductive approach may be useful in devising a typology of conflict responses, it may limit the types of responses considered or suggest types seldom used. Inductive approaches may produce a more representative typology of strategies for dealing with conflict in intimate relationships.

Attempts to create a typology of cognitive responses to dissatisfaction using inductive methods have been reported in the research literature. Kipnis (1976) listed 44 different perceived responses to conflict. Subjecting these responses to factor analysis, Fitzpatrick and Winke (1979) identified five underlying strategies or dimensions: manipulation, nonnegotiation, emotional appeal, empathic understanding, and strategy of personal rejection. Rands et al. (1981) asked 244 California married couples to respond to questions about the kinds of conflicts they encountered, their conflict style, their expected outcome of the conflict, and their marital satisfaction. Four main ways of dealing with conflict were found that varied along dimensions of perceived aggressiveness and intimacy:

> A nonintimate–aggressive strategy, about 30% of the respondents: least satisfying especially when the partner was seen as uncompromising;
>
> A nonintimate–nonaggressive strategy, about 20% of the respondents: in this subtype, some spouses appeared to tolerate their relationship rather well, even though it was unexciting;
>
> An intimate–aggressive strategy, about 20% of the respondents: for some of the spouses in this subtype who achieved intimacy after a confrontation, spouses' high intimacy seemed to counteract perception of their attacking behavior.
>
> An intimate–nonaggressive strategy, about 30% of the respondents, which couples found the most satisfying.

The researchers found that perceptions of conflict outcome varied from one extreme in which less intimacy was perceived following the conflict and the other in which the spouses felt closer, thought they understood each other better, reported having fun making up, and said they tended to compromise. It is interesting to note that Rands and her colleagues observed that a high percentage

(70%) of the couples in their study tended to deal with conflict situations by selecting less intimate and more aggressive strategies that resulted in little, if any, satisfaction.

In other attempts to examine cognitive responses to sources of conflict, Rusbult and Zembrodt (1983) asked 50 undergraduate men and women to write essays in which they described their responses to dissatisfying romantic relationships. Then, 200 undergraduate men and women judged the degree of similarity among these descriptions. Results suggested a typology including four strategies (if asked what respondents would do or intend to do) and as perceived response categories (if asked what respondents actually did or observed their partners doing):

Exit. Divorce, break up, and separate.

Voice. Attempt to change the relationship, discuss problems, compromise, work things out, and adopt a problem-solving orientation.

Loyalty. Accept minor problems, commit to maintaining the relationship, and assume that conditions will improve.

Neglect. Ignore the partner, not care about the relationship, and allow conditions to worsen.

As so often happens when researchers attempt to devise a typology, there were mixed cases in which partners preferred strategies typical of more than one category.

Rusbult's typology relates to social exchange theory in the following ways: When partners are satisfied with their relationship (rewards outweigh costs), perceive no superior alternatives to their primary relationship, make high investments in a relationship, and perceive social pressures to remain in the relationship, partners prefer to be loyal or give voice as alternative cognitive responses to perceived sources of conflict. The greater the satisfaction, investments, and social pressures to remain together, and the more inferior the alternatives, the more the partners are committed to the relationship, and the more likely they are to respond with voice rather than loyalty.

However, when partners are not satisfied with their relationship (costs outweigh rewards), perceive superior alternatives to their primary relationship, have not made investments in a relationship, and perceive no social pressures to remain in the relationship, partners prefer to neglect or exit from the relationship as alternative cognitive responses to perceived sources of conflict. The lesser the satisfaction, investments, social pressures to remain together, and the more superior the alternatives, the less the partners are committed to the relationship, and the more likely they are to respond by exiting rather than with neglect.

Building on Rusbult's typology of responses to conflict, Healey and Bell (1990) argue that partners may progress through different types of cognition as dissatisfaction grows. At first they might prefer loyalty as a strategy, hoping that things will get better soon. They may turn to the strategy of giving voice when the situation does not improve, then may decide to neglect the partner when that fails, and eventually may choose to exit the relationship. By combining Healey and Bell's notion of progression with social exchange theory, it might be argued that newly formed couples would prefer loyalty because they fear losing their partner, who is not fully committed to the relationship. However, after commitment takes place, they prefer to give voice to their dissatisfaction, but if conditions only worsen, then they prefer neglect. Finally, when superior alternatives appear, they prefer to exit. Longitudinal research could be designed to study cognitive responses to sources of conflict as a dynamic process over time.

Rusbult's typology of self-reported strategies includes "giving voice" as one of the four general responses to perceived sources of conflict. Does giving voice itself involve alternative communication strategies as cognitive responses? Since the early 1980s, researchers in psychology and communication have employed self-reports for assessing specific conflict communication strategies. These strategies consist of perceived or intended conflict communication behaviors often referred to as "communication tactics" because (1) they are not enacted behavioral responses but rather cognitive responses, (2) they are not observed by objective raters but rather reported by the intimate partners involved in the conflict, and (3) they are not observed at the time of their occurrence but rather recalled after the event, or intended in the future.

Margolin, Fernandez, Gorin, and Ortiz (1982) created a conflict inventory (CI) consisting of 26 tactics distributed over three scales: Constructive problem solving (e.g., "listen attentively to what your partner is saying"), aggression (e.g., "insult your partner or call him or her names"), and withdrawal (e.g., "sulk or pout"). The measure discriminated between nondistressed and distressed partners and correlated well with Straus's (1977) Conflict Tactics Scale. Kahn, Coyne, and Margolin (1985) showed that the measure is useful for assessing either one's own conflict communication strategy (recalled or intended) or one's perception of a partner's strategy (recalled).

Canary and his colleagues devised a self-report consisting of constructive/integrative, destructive/distributive, and avoidance conflict communication strategies based on those reported by Cupach (1982) and conflict communication behaviors observed by Sillars (1980a, 1980b). The three strategies consisted of 47 communication tactics. Canary and Spitzberg (1989) found that integrative/constructive communication strategies were positively related to scores on a perceived communication competence questionnaire, whereas distributive/destructive and avoidance communication strategies were negatively associated with communication competence.

More recently, Canary, Cunningham, and Cody (1988) asked 434 college students at three western universities to describe a "recent" conflict and indicate the degree to which they recalled using each of the 47 communication tactics. Factor analysis of the data produced seven conflict communication strategies: integrative (e.g., "I sought a mutually beneficial solution"), personal criticism of the partner (e.g., "I criticized an aspect of his or her personality"), showing anger (e.g., "I shouted at him or her"), sarcasm (e.g., "I was sarcastic in my use of humor"), topic shifting (e.g., "I avoided the issue"), semantic focus (e.g., "I focused on the meaning of the words more than the conflict issue"), and extended denial (e.g., "I denied that there was any problem or conflict"). Using 97 dyads consisting of college students and "partners" with whom they had experienced a conflict with the past two weeks, Canary and Spitzberg (1990) used the 7-factor version of their instrument and found that the partners most readily recalled one another's use of two conflict communication strategies; anger and criticism.

Modes or Conflict Management Styles

One line of research on alternative strategies for managing conflict in intimate relationships actually grew out of business administration/management research and a concern for supervisor–subordinate conflicts in industrial organizations. Arguing that the competitive–cooperative dichotomy was too limited, Blake and Mouton (1964) proposed a typology for the management of organizational conflict, consisting of the following five strategies: avoiding, smoothing, forcing, compromising, and confronting.

These conflict management strategies (CMS) may be related to social exchange theory in terms of rewards and costs.

Avoiding (lose–lose). Seeing nothing to gain by engaging in conflict, individuals avoid it. Consequently, both parties lose out on obtaining any rewards.

Smoothing (lose–win). Individuals perceive that they have nothing to gain by continuing a conflict and that the other party can receive rewards if they simply give in. Thus, they acquiesce.

Forcing (win–lose). Individuals perceive that they can gain an advantage over the other party through conflict and compete until they win.

Compromising (win & lose). Individuals perceive that they must make trade-offs (sacrifice some rewards to gain others) when in conflict; so they settle for a compromise.

Confronting (win–win). Individuals perceive that engaging in conflict will result in both parties getting the rewards they want.

In a series of studies, these conflict management strategies were measured with one-item scales (Renwick, 1977), a set of proverbs (Burke, 1970; Lawrence & Lorsch, 1967), and Blake and Mouton's managerial grid (Bernardin & Alvarez, 1976; Zammuto, London, & Rowland, 1979). According to Kilmann and Thomas (1977), these measures are subject to serious criticism.

Reinterpreting the original five conflict management styles, Kilmann and Thomas reported on the development of the Management of Differences Exercise (MODE instrument) (Kilmann & Thomas, 1977; Thomas & Kilmann, 1974). The above five styles were renamed as competing (forcing), collaborating (confronting), accommodating (smoothing), avoiding, and compromising modes, which presumably indicate two underlying dimensions: assertiveness and cooperativeness. To ascertain an individual's preference or intention to use one of these conflict management styles, the Thomas-Kilmann measure structured 60 questions into 30 either/or responses. The forced choices for the given conflict styles were paired with the conflict styles three times in a manner that allowed a comparison among the modes an equal number of times. This forced choice pairing resulted in a five-scale measure with an expected intercorrelation between scales of –.25. The measure did not correlate significantly with social desirability which suggested that something other than social expectations was reflected by the measure. Evidence for the validity of the instrument was provided by Kilmann and Thomas (1977).

According to Rahim (1983), Kilmann and Thomas (1977) used a small and nonrandom sample of students to test the reliability and validity of the MODE instrument. Moreover, Rahim argued that their study did not provide evidence for the independence of the five factors or conflict modes. To overcome these limitations, Rahim reinterpreted the original five conflict styles as dominating (forcing), integrating (confronting), obliging (smoothing), avoiding, and compromising styles and relabeled the two basic dimensions, concern for self and concern for others. The first dimension explained the degree (high or low) to which a person attempts to satisfy his or her own concerns; the second explained the degree (high or low) to which a person wants to satisfy the concerns of others (Rahim & Bonoma, 1979). When the two dimensions were graphed onto a matrix, they yielded the five modes that may be defined in terms of exchange (see Cosier & Ruble, 1981).

Using students, teachers, school administrators, and hospital management personnel as respondents, Rahim devised three separate versions of his instrument differing only in reference to conflict with boss, subordinate, or peer. He then used a national sample consisting of 1,219 randomly selected executives, representing top, middle, and lower organizational levels in 25 different industries. Factor analyses of these data reflected quite clearly the five conflict management styles. Rahim reported acceptable levels of test reliability and provided evidence in support for its validity. While four of the five scales were free from response bias such as social desirability (Crowne & Marlowe, 1960), there was a marginal but significant positive correlation between social desirability (SD) and the integrating scales. Rahim suggested ways to control for SD should it be considered a problem. Since the Rahim measure used business executives as respondents when developing the instrument, he recommended that the measure be used to diagnose styles of handing conflict only among members of business organizations.

Although the usefulness of the MODE instrument and Rahim's 5-factor measure for studying conflict in other contexts remains questionable, a few researchers have applied them or advocated their use in intimate contexts. At least one practicing therapist claims that an understanding of the five conflict modes contributes to effective reality therapy for spouses in conflict (Hallock, 1988). Berryman-Fink and Brunner (1987), Chusmir and Mills (1989), Hallock (1988), Mills and Chusmir (1988), Pistole (1989), Rosenthal and Hautaluoma (1988), and Shockley-Zalabak and Morley (1984) have used either the Thomas-Kilmann measure or the Rahim instrument to study how conflict is managed in male–female intimate relationships. However, using the measure to generalize to intimate relationships may be a questionable practice. Specifying different targets (including parent, friend, and sibling), Hammock, Richardson, Pilkington, and Utley (1990) found that a 4-factor solution was more appropriate for nonorganizational contexts than the 5-factor solution discovered by Rahim. In their study, the items comprising Rahim's integrating and compromising factors loaded on a single factor, while the remaining factors were identical to his. Thus, when collecting data in nonorganizational settings, they recommend modifying Rahim's instrument by combining the integrating and compromising factors into a single one.

Which Conflict Management Strategies Contribute Most to Intimate Relationship Satisfaction and Commitment?

As indicated in Chapter 1, research conducted within the cognitive–exchange perspective examines the role played by partners' cognitions (i.e., self–other perceptions and conflict management strategies) in relationship development. Questions of interest are among the following: What antecedent conditions influence one's choice of conflict management strategy? What alternative strategies are best for dealing with different sources of conflict? To the extent that dissatisfaction plays a role in dissolution, researchers offer conflicting answers to these questions.

Earlier in this chapter, dissatisfaction was identified as an outcome as well as a source of conflict. It is also possible that the choice of strategy for managing conflict in long-term intimate relationships also adds to satisfaction that contributes to relationship development. Researchers take sides on the issue regarding whether confrontation strategies result in greater relationship satisfaction than do avoidance strategies.

A number of scholars argue in favor of open confrontation:

> *Navran (1967) found that marital satisfaction correlated with "good" communication at .82. Satisfied partners usually discussed most matters, stopped the communication less often (e.g., by sulking), discussed more often personal matters, used more words with a private meaning, could more easily predict the type of day the partner had, and*

communicated more nonverbally (e.g., by exchange of glances).

In the case where unresolved problems may undermine a relationship, some researchers see the direct resolution of conflict as potentially increasing partner interdependence and intimacy (see Scanzoni, 1979b).

Genshaft (1980) found that dissatisfied couples see their partners as more defensive than satisfied spouses.

Knudson, Sommers, and Golding (1980) have obtained data from couples who resolve conflicts by engaging the issues and from those who avoid dealing with sources of conflict. Results show that open discussion by itself offers valuable outcomes such as increased agreement and increased understanding of the partner's perceptions. For partners who avoid issues and conflicts, there are negative outcomes such as decreased agreement and increased discrepancies between partners' perceptions.

The results of several studies reveal that confronting the problem of inequity and restoring equity in an intimate relationship produces greater relationship satisfaction (e.g., Sabatelli & Cecil-Pigo, 1985; Ting-Toomey, 1984; Utne et al., 1984).

Canary and Spitzberg (1987) link confrontation and avoidance strategies to sources of conflict with partners' ratings of appropriateness in both same-sex friendships and opposite-sex relationships. Their results show that integrative strategies such as disclosure and cooperation in the form of problem solving are considered more appropriate in both the same-sex and opposite-sex relationships than avoidance or distributive strategies that are perceived to be antagonistic and competitive.

Acitelli (1988) has asked 42 married couples the question: What effect does couples' talking about their relationship have on spouses' feelings of contentment. She has found that relationship talk has a positive effect on partners' feelings of contentment.

Cloven and Roloff (1991) claim that "mulling" over problems increases the severity of perceived conflicts and the likelihood that partners choose to place the blame for the problem on them. In their research on college roommates, they found that attempts to talk over their relationship problems attenuated the negative effects of prolonged thought.

Crohan (1992) found that black couples and white couples who believe in avoiding conflicts reported lower marital happiness in the first year of marriage and again 2 years later than those couples in which both spouses believe in confronting conflicts.

Although some studies argue for direct and open confrontation or against avoidance, there is evidence that at times avoidance is associated with relationship satisfaction.

Fitzpatrick and Winke (1979) observed that highly satisfied couples were more likely than less satisfied couples to use the strategy of manipulation to avoid open conflict. Pike and Sillars (1985) also have found in their study of couples' conflict behavior that conflict avoidance was used to a greater extent by more satisfied than dissatisfied couples.

Confrontation may have disastrous consequences if it turns into a heated argument that gets out of hand. As presented above, Rands et al. (1981) describe a nonintimate–aggressive pattern that expands to include other issues. In such cases, once hostility is expressed by either partner, Gaelick et al. (1985) show that it is likely to be perceived by a couple as growing in frequency over the course of the interaction. Similarly, Menaghan (1982) links the problems to the choice of coping efforts suggesting the perception of a worsening spiral.

Some couples cannot cope with additional problems. Menaghan concludes that sometimes, as problems mount, *typical coping choices may actually exacerbate distress and relationship problems. Moreover, according to Menaghan (1982), the question whether to confront problems is complicated by feelings of distress and the actual resolution of problems. She found that two nonconfrontational strategies for coping with marital problems, selective ignoring and resignation, increased ongoing distress and had little impact on the problem later. The confrontational strategy of negotiation did not reduce feelings of distress but was associated with fewer problems later. Only the nonconfrontational strategy of "optimistic comparisons" was associated with both lower distress and fewer later problems. Thus, to reduce distress now and later, optimistic comparison is recommended.*

Many conflict researchers who advocate confrontation assume that increased agreement and improved understanding are associated with relationship satisfaction. Research questions this assumption. Research on "spousal consensus" shows that happier, more satisfied marriages may have less accurate understandings of spouses' areas of disagreements than do inferior marriages (Booth & Welch, 1978; Levinger & Breedlove, 1966; Luckey, 1962; Neal & Groat, 1976). According to Sillars, Pike, Jones, and Murphy (1984), there is a moderate correlation between marital satisfaction and perceived agreement but not between satisfaction and actual agreement or empathy. Thus, in regard to marital stability and satisfaction, sometimes it may be better to "let sleeping dogs lie."

Several researchers have shown that, perhaps out of fear that conflict will destroy a couple's relationship, avoidance is the norm for dealing with conflict in American life. Some of this research has demonstrated the following:

Using a color matching test that created instances of disagreement between partners (Ryder & Goodrich, 1966) and using the revealed differences form (Strodtbeck, 1951), researchers were surprised by the tendency of spouses to avoid conflicts by giving wrong answers. Conscious or unconscious denial, distortion, misperception, and lying seemed to be common ways to avoid disagreements. Thus, spouses faced with apparent discrepancies between them tended to reinterpret the situation in order to demonstrate that there was "really" no disagreement between them.

Over a period of 5 days, Birchler et al. (1975) observed that spouses engaged in an average of 13 behaviors that were displeasurable to their partners, but that they had only one argument.

Banks, Altendorf, Greene, and Cody (1987) have observed that avoidance is a common type of disengagement strategy.

In their review of the literature on the "chilling effect," Roloff and Cloven (1990) concluded that there was a tendency in intimate relationships like marriage for partners to avoid dealing with conflicts.

Baxter and Dindia (1990) have found that inward withdrawal and problem avoidance were among the common strategies used by intimate partners to maintain their relationship.

In conclusion, intentionally avoiding the discussion of conflict issues appears to be a typical response to sources of conflict. Whether it is the best strategy is still open to question.

Rusbult and her colleagues have labeled some alternative responses to conflict as constructive and others as destructive. They either (1) asked students to write how they would deal with dissatisfaction in their romantic relationships and then coded the answers (e.g., Rusbult et al., 1982) or (2) asked them to select alternatives that have been devised to reflect the exit, voice, loyalty, and neglect typology (Rusbult et al., 1986b). The researchers compared respondents' answers with partners' estimation of how the respondents would answer and reported the following correlations: exit (.53), voice (.34), loyalty (.30) and neglect (.42). Dissatisfaction was associated most with exit and least with voice and loyalty. Rusbult and her colleagues claimed that two dimensions, constructiveness–destructiveness and activity–passivity, underlie the alternative responses to conflict. Voice and loyalty were believed to represent constructive strategies; exit and neglect were determined to be destructive.

There are situations, however, in which neglect and exit might be viewed as positive, while voice and loyalty might have negative consequences. Research needs to tie down the conditions under which it is better to respond one way than another. In any case, Rusbult is open to a variety of alternative strategies when responding to conflict and sees some as more likely than others to produce relationship dissatisfaction.

Because confrontation may be a good idea sometimes but harmful at other times, many cognitive–exchange scholars are advocating alternative conflict management strategies, ranging from confrontation to avoidance, depending on the situation.

When Are Partners Likely to Confront or Avoid Conflict?

Presumably, there are factors that contribute to confrontation or avoidance proneness. Among the factors that appear to fit this model are commitment, power, family strengths, issue salience, sex/gender, and context.

Commitment. Research shows that those who are not yet committed to a relationship prefer more conflict avoidance than partners at later stages in their romantic relationships. For those who exhibited the most commitment to a romantic relationship (i.e., the married), Fitzpatrick and Winke (1979) report that they are more likely to utilize the open conflict strategies of emotional appeal or personal rejection to gain their way, while those who espouse the least commitment to the relationship (e.g., casual dating) indicate that they prefer to use the conflict avoidance strategies of manipulation and nonnegotiation. Moreover, more securely attached dating partners report higher relational satisfaction and are more likely to engage in constructive problem-solving strategies (Pistole, 1989).

Power. Intimate partners who perceive a balance of power in their relationships are likely to prefer strategies that confront issues, whereas power imbalances tend to produce a preference for avoidance strategies. In imbalanced relationships, powerful partners may be expected to confront, while powerless partners are expected to choose avoidance strategies. One form of confrontation avoidance is the "chilling effect" as a sign of "powerlessness" (Roloff & Cloven, 1990). Power is viewed here as the chance to influence the behavior of others in accord with one's own wishes. Hocker and Wilmot (1985) suggest that some partners downgrade their requests prior to making them simply because they anticipate negative reactions from their more powerful counterparts. Further, they may be inhibited from even initiating influence attempts, the essence of the chilling effect. As such they meet the following conditions: They focus on interests that have a negative impact on their partners, they withhold comments on these interests from their partners, and they are afraid that confrontation would damage the relationship.

While "powerlessness" may influence the extent to which one is likely to confront a partner, interestingly, it may also be seen as an outcome of uncommitted relationships. Clearly, the chilling effect is most likely to occur when a relationship is perceived to be unstable (or lacking in commitment), an important condition that specifies when differences in power have the greatest effect.

Family Strengths. Because some intimate partners feel better prepared to deal with sources of conflict, they are more likely than others to prefer confrontational strategies. Rusbult, Johnson, and Morrow (1986a) report that greater prior satisfaction with a relationship and greater investment of resources predispose partners to respond with voice or loyalty and to avoid reacting with exit or neglect. Similarly, intimate partners who are satisfied with their family and quality of life prefer to discuss their differences (MacKinnon, MacKinnon, & Franken, 1984).

Issue Salience, Number, and Severity of Problems. When the issue is more important, intimate partners choose different strategies for handling the conflict than when issues are minor. Administrating a conflict measure to 59 men and 55 women, Rosenthal and Hautaluoma (1988) have obtained data showing a greater preference for collaboration and competition and lesser preference for accommodation and avoidance in conflicts over more important issues.

The severity and number of problems also are a factor in some cases. Menaghan (1982) has discovered that the number of current marital problems is strongly predictive of coping strategies: People with more problems are less likely to prefer negotiation or more likely to choose "optimistic comparisons" (i.e., view one's situation relative to the past and relative to one's peers), selective ignoring, and resignation. Further support is offered by Rusbult et al. (1986a), who observe that greater problem severity encourages preference for exit and voice strategies and discourages loyalty and neglect.

Sex and Gender. Research on conflict management strategies in male–female intimate relationships is contradictory. Studies finding support for male–female differences are Berryman-Fink and Brunner (1987), Fitzpatrick and Winke (1979), Kilmann and Thomas (1977), Rahim (1983), Roloff and Greenberg (1979), Shockley-Zalabak and Morley (1984) for student respondents only, and Zammuto, London, and Rowland (1979). Studies failing to find such differences in preference for conflict management strategies are Chusmir and Mills (1989), Renwick (1977), Shockley-Zalabak and Morley (1984) for nonstudent respondents only, and Sternberg and Soriano (1984).

Although the results are contradictory and difficult to interpret, a few points may be made about the effects of sex and gender differences on the selection of conflict management strategies. For overall conflict in marriage, men are more likely than women to want to blame their spouse (Kleinke, 1977). Moreover, research shows that men prefer to avoid emotional involvement in conflict situations more than do women (Kelley et al., 1978). Rusbult et al. (1986b) report that men respond to the sources of conflict with less preference for voice and loyalty strategies and more for neglect and exit than do women.

Men do not always avoid confronting their partners, however. When they do confront them, research shows that men tend to select more coercive, competitive, aggressive, and antisocial strategies as responses to conflict, while women prefer more compromising (Berryman-Fink & Brunner, 1987), less aggressive (Margolin, 1987), and more prosocial strategies (Roloff & Greenberg, 1979). In comparing preferences for conflict management strategies of college students versus employees, Shockley-Zalabak and Morley (1984) found that only in the student sample did men tend to seek self-interests and women tend to be more other-oriented; in the working world these differences were not found. At home, however, the responses of men and women to the sources of conflict tended to conform to stereotypes of male–female social behavior (Kelley et al., 1978; Kleinke, 1977) derived from American historical experience (Goldner, 1985).

Personality. Do individuals prefer the same confrontation–avoidance strategy across situations? Research has produced a complex answer to this question. Individuals were found to be quite consistent in their conflict management strategies both within and across content domains (Sternberg & Soriano, 1984). This suggests that each conflict management strategy is a personal style or trait that one has regardless of the situation. For example, Pete sees himself as competitive in all conflict situations. Moreover, while strong consistencies in conflict management strategies are observed by individuals across different situations, widespread differences are observed across individuals (Sternberg & Dobson, 1987). This means that people may tend to prefer to use the same strategy regardless of the situation, but different people have different preferences for conflict management strategies. So, Mary (who sees herself as collaborative across conflict situations) is different from Pete (who sees himself as competitive) and tends to see herself as being so regardless of the person with whom she is in conflict.

Other lines of research have reported that personality variables are associated with at least three of the conflict management strategies—namely, confronting, smoothing, and forcing. Bell and Blakeney (1977) linked confronting to achievement motivation and forcing to aggression. In addition, Jones and Melcher (1982) find positive correlations between affiliation and smoothing, deference and forcing, succorance and smoothing, nurturing and smoothing, dogmatism and confronting, and Machiavellianism and confronting. Negative correlations are reported for affiliation and forcing as well as Machiavellianism and smoothing. Finally, Sternberg and Soriano (1984) predict quite well the choice of conflict management strategy from knowledge of certain intellectual and personality characteristics.

Other researchers are also finding that confrontation and avoidance may be viewed as personality traits. For example, some people have a trait of argumentativeness, whereas others prefer to avoid arguments (Infante & Rancer, 1982).

Cultural Influence. Strategies for dealing with conflicts are influenced by couples' cultural heritage (Cahn, 1985). The American value for individual freedom and economic competition encourages a win–lose or competitive orientation toward dealing with conflicts. However, the Japanese value for group harmony and dependence on others encourages accommodation. In fact, Prunty, Klopf, and Ishii (1990) found that Japanese have a significantly weaker argumentativeness trait than Americans.

Context. While studies indicate that there are gender, cultural, and personal pressures to confront or avoid conflict, partners may use different conflict management strategies in social and organizational contexts. Specifically, researchers have found that people who hold supervisory positions in the workplace prefer to use different strategies at home and at work. Mills and Chusmir (1988), for example, have found that there was a tendency among 221 managers at three different organizational levels to prefer a more accommodating and collaborational strategy at home than in the workplace. In a follow-up study, Chusmir and Mills (1989) reported that there was a tendency among 201 male and female managers to prefer more competitive strategies of conflict resolution when dealing with workers and more accommodating strategies with their partner at home.

The cognitive–exchange approach accounts for a great deal of empirical research on intimates in conflict, and it also offers techniques for helping intimate partners deal with the sources of conflicts as they arise.

EDUCATING INTIMATE PARTNERS ABOUT HOW TO MANAGE CONFLICTS

In Chapters 2 and 3, specific techniques and suggestions for helping couples resolve conflicts were presented because they were consistent with the dominant research paradigms discussed in those chapters. In Chapter 2, behavior modification techniques and specific conflict communication skills training were presented because they conform to the assumptions made by the systems–interactionist approach. In Chapter 3, rule creation and enforcement techniques were recommended for mediators because they conform to the assumptions made by the rules–interventionist paradigm. In this chapter, cognitive techniques are described because they conform to the assumptions made by the cognitive–exchange approach.

From a cognitive–exchange perspective, how might the potential for conflict be reduced? When sources of conflict arise, what is the best cognitive response to make? When intimate partners prefer to "give voice" to their concerns, how should they go about it?

How Might the Potential for Conflict Be Reduced?

According to the cognitive–exchange approach, some of the sources of conflict result from faulty perceptions or inferences (Weiss et al.,

1973). Without intervening to alter faulty perceptions, unrealistic expectations, and faulty inferences, intimate partners' training is unlikely to have much impact. Training in cognitive restructuring, a method that fits within the cognitive–exchange paradigm, helps intimate partners deal with sources of conflicts and improve intimacy.

Essentially, cognitive restructuring is a means of increasing relationship satisfaction by relabeling "faulty" cognition (i.e., misperception and unwarranted inference) (Jacobson & Margolin, 1979). Before partners can engage in effective problem solving, faulty cognition needs correction. Of particular interest are perceptions of undesirable behavior and inferences made from them. For example, a spouse may acknowledge that his or her behavior may be responsible for a partner's dissatisfaction. At the same time, however, he or she may challenge the partner's inferences because people may misinterpret the reasons for one another's behavior. Moreover, a partner may reinterpret the behavior in a way that casts it in a more positive light. For example, one's spouse who suspected a partner of trying to avoid the other may be made to realize that the partner is staying at the office each night to earn more money to provide a better standard of living for them both.

The most sweeping changes in the treatment of marital problems include not only communication training, but also cognitive restructuring techniques (Jacobson, 1978). Cognitive restructuring may be used to align partners' feelings about each other. Many partners need to realize that their feelings about one another depend on their behavior toward each other (Fincham & Bradbury, 1991). Once partners see the connection between their positive feelings and the other's behavior, they may see the necessity for acting more often in ways that appear more loving to the partner.

Cognitive restructuring is useful as a means for converting unrealistic into realistic expectations. Because unrealistic expectations stem from utopian views of intimate relationships, identifying myths may help intimate partners to value instead a "real relationship" in which partners openly discuss and negotiate their interests, goals, and desires.

Intimate partners may benefit from adopting more positive expectations through cognitive restructuring. It is important to maintain positive expectancies regarding the partner's behaviors. A couple may learn how to place recent negative events in a more positive perspective, by emphasizing the positive elements in the week rather than dwelling on the negative. Since the goal is to increase both a couple's exchange of rewarding behaviors and subjective feelings of satisfaction with the relationship, it is helpful for intimate partners to emphasize the positive aspects of their relationship.

Another way in which individual perceptions may benefit from cognitive restructuring concerns the fact that spouses have different perspectives. Frequently, they fail to perceive their own contributions to the conflict and view change as a unilateral venture. They also may not understand "where the partner is coming from." Thus, learning empathy is helpful.

Cognitive restructuring may involve changing partners' conception of problem-solving discussions. To successfully resolve problems, partners need to see the value of adopting a mutual orientation or a collaborative set, enacted in the form of cooperative behaviors. Partners need to see the reward value of working together toward change. Earlier in this chapter, sources of conflict are identified as barriers to rewards. If constructive confrontation helps resolve the conflict and produce greater intimacy, any attempt to induce partners to more openly confront, discuss, and cooperate to resolve sources of conflict must be accompanied by an emphasis on the benefits that may accrue to them as a result of collaboration.

Accommodation Strategy as Avoidance

There are times when it may be best not to take a stand on an issue or to assert one's needs, interests, goals, or values. For example, one may encounter the problem of having a partner who does not change or permit one to change because such changes threaten the partner's core values, interests, or needs. In other words, permitting another the freedom to grow may be viewed as self-destructive by one's partner. Such people desire to maintain a particular situation because they find it personally satisfying, even though it prevents change and interferes with the personal satisfaction and growth of the partner. When one's partner behaves this way, cognitive restructuring may produce strategies of accommodation (e.g., Rusbult's alternative conflict management strategy of remaining loyal) that are useful in the maintenance of an otherwise successful relationship or when one has no alternative at present. Two useful accommodation strategies are productive ambiguity and the reorganization of one's priorities (Cahn, 1987).

One way to accommodate a partner is *productive ambiguity*—by not making clear his or her own interests or concerns. Consider the situation in which a wife enjoys sailing more than her husband, who chooses not to make his aversion to sailing known. Productive ambiguity may be useful and productive if the situation meets the following conditions. First, the issue may be important to her. In such a case, if the husband openly criticizes her sailing interests, he could upset her and appear less supportive and attractive to her, and she might withdraw from him. Second, the issue may not be very important to him. If he does not object to a few sailing artifacts around the house, and a sailing trip once a year or so, perhaps she may feel satisfied. Finally, the issue may be tolerated if it does not require actual action by both partners. If he thinks that her sailing interests have little likelihood of involving him because they do not have a sailboat or they do not live near water, then he may simply let the matter ride. Although this strategy is not completely honest in that he fails to make an issue out of their differences in regard to sailing, it results in a measure of support on a matter that may be best left alone. Thus, it is not enough to identify perceived rewards; one must weigh them against costs if partners openly confront one another.

There are times when it is best to reorganize one's priorities—to change, eliminate, or reorder one or more of one's own interests, values, or goals. Although many people have difficulty believing this, it is possible for one to perceive more or less of one's own need, value, or interest. At any rate, a relationship is most likely to survive when marital partners strive for balance, attempt to be reasonable, and try to proportion their interests in a manner that fits the expectations of their partners. For example, one spouse may like to watch particular television programs late at night, while the other spouse prefers to go to bed and get up early. By setting a VCR to record the late-night programs, both spouses can go to bed and get up at a "reasonable hour."

A reorganization of one's priorities is not necessarily bad. Sometimes people find that they prefer it. As they find themselves more open to new interests and different people, individuals may develop new personalities and become more interesting as partners.

When Intimate Partners Find It Appropriate to "Give Voice" to Their Concerns, How Can They Be Effective?

Remer and de Mesquita (1990) have developed a six-stage model for constructively confronting a partner: preparation, lead-in, confrontation, active listening, negotiation, and follow-up. They explain in detail each of these stages and suggest techniques for successful and effective performance of each stage.

Central to confrontation is effective communication which is used to convey to the partner information about one's needs, interests, objectives, and expectations (Scanzoni, 1979b). Accuracy is important—one's conveying as precisely as possible what he or she actually intends to communicate, and others grasping this intent as accurately as possible. As Levinger (1979) has observed, potential partners initially exchange services and information that are valued generally (in a universal sense), and later they will exchange more valued rewards that signify unique meaning to the partners (in a particular sense). As part of a "working through" process, each partner increases his or her knowledge of the other and builds a more accurate cognitive picture of the other person that facilitates more accurate predicting to unexplored areas of interaction.

As partners become more intimate, they can deal with potential conflicts of interest long before they become serious problems later by asserting themselves when issues first arise and by effectively listening to their partner (Cahn, 1987). They can also use these same techniques when confronting problems to clarify their perspectives.

Clarification of Perceptions

Self-assertion or disclosure refers to one's ability to convey to others her or his cognition (e.g., intention, interest, and concern). Self-assertion enables one to make known to a partner his or her feelings, wants, needs, interests, and intentions. Improvement in self-assertion better enables another to develop clear expectations toward one's actions.

Listening reflects one's ability to identify an internal state or cognition in others. Effective listening and checking out are necessary for accurately perceiving a partner's intent, interest, or concern. Primarily a matter of paying attention, effective listening consists of strategies that better enable people to pay attention to one another (Aronson, 1974; Murphy, 1987; Nichols & Stevens, 1957). In addition, there are techniques that assist listening, such as checking out the partner by asking for clarification of his or her internal state (Miller, Nunnally, & Wackman, 1975). Through training, intimate partners need to be exposed to these ideas and to change their listening behavior.

CONCLUSION

According to cognitive–exchange researchers, intimacy, alternative attractions, conflict management, and sources of conflict are separately included in a framework of perceived rewards and costs (including investments and social pressures). In this framework, comparison levels and comparison levels for alternatives are internal (cognitive) processes that determine intimate relationship development as measured by self-reported relationship satisfaction and commitment. Relationship development (a more rewarding relationship) is clearly distinguished from relationship dissolution (a more costly relationship). In addition, the framework includes conflict management by confrontation or avoidance of sources of conflict by cognitive restructuring, productive ambiguity, reorganization of one's priorities, and clarification of perspectives.

It appears to be the case that at times cognitive constructs help to explain and predict intimate relationship development (Heider, 1958; Kelley, 1971). According to Fincham et al. (1990), Kelley (1979), and Kelley et al. (1983), in using social exchange to formulate a comprehensive theory of conflict in intimate relationships, one should take into consideration the actor's thoughts and feelings that give rise to conflict. The emergence of studies on perceptual factors also points to the importance of thoughts and feelings for understanding conflict behavior (e.g., Braiker & Kelley, 1979; Fincham et al. 1990; Kelley, 1979; Orvis, Kelley, & Butler, 1976; Sillars, 1980a, 1980b).

Cognitive–exchange theories often rely on self-reports to define operational procedures for making data-based predictions. Operational definitions in the form of self-reports exist for measuring perceived rewards, costs (including investments), availability of alternative relationships, general and specific sources of conflict, perceptions and inferences, relationship dissatisfaction, and conflict management strategies. However, some self-reports include measures of abstract variables. As Margolin (1990) points out, abstract variables require more inference to rate and study them, reducing reliability and making it difficult to know whether the variables actually have been measured. The abstraction problem is particularly relevant for the concept of dissatisfaction (see critique by Fincham & Bradbury, 1987b).

In spite of the elaborate design for collecting data, Rusbult's concept of "giving voice" as a response to relationship dissatisfaction is also ambiguous. Communication scholars have identified a number of patterns that intimate partners use when "giving voice" to problems, complaints, and dissatisfaction. For example, Alberts (1990) and Newton and Burgoon (1990) have found subtle patterns involving the use of humor as well as perceptions of verbal behavior and nonverbal cues that intimate partners use to "give voice" to their conflicts. Margolin, Fernandez, Gorin, and Ortiz (1982) and Canary and Spitzberg (1990) have developed instruments for measuring different conflict communication strategies. These studies show that "giving voice" may involve the use of alternative communication strategies and tactics that vary in their directness and effectiveness.

Conflict-related research on intimate partners from a cognitive–exchange perspective relies heavily on subjective and recalled perceptions and affect. As interesting and useful as behavioral data might be, it would be impractical to attempt to video/audiotape and code interactions of a sufficient number of relationships as they first form, grow, and perhaps disintegrate over a number of years. It is more practical to devise global measures that partners themselves may use to assess the relationship and the handling of conflict overall. In addition, most partners would object to having their private life videotaped for posterity. Some intimate behaviors are too private to permit direct methods of observation. In such cases, a researcher is fortunate to have respondents who are at least willing to answer a limited number of questions about their intimate behavior. Finally, the cognitive–exchange perspective has found it necessary to include people's thoughts, feelings, and attributions to adequately explain the relationship between conflict and the development or deterioration of intimacy. These subjective experiences are frequently accessible only through self-reporting techniques. For example, some researchers believe that the only way to ascertain what is troubling intimate partners is to ask them (i.e., self-report). Therefore, by virtue of the data sought and due to the nature of some of the variables, this type of analysis must rely heavily on subjective, often retrospective data obtained by self-reports in the form of questionnaires.

As useful as they are, data derived from self-report measures have not always enjoyed the level of acceptance achieved by data obtained through objective behavioral observation. Often, self-report measures are criticized because of the likelihood of response bias and lack of behavioral data.

Response Bias. Even if one grants the argument that it is the perception of behaviors and not necessarily the behaviors themselves that have effects, a problem of response bias still arises when respondents are asked to subjectively assess at one time satisfaction, rewards–costs, alternative attractions, commitment, and responses to dissatisfaction because connections among these constructs are made inside the mind of the participant. A negative feeling about one (such as relationship satisfaction) tends to influence other, if not all, aspects of a relationship. Also, responses may differ in social desirability.

One way to investigate the role of subjective distortions in the self-reporting process is to include both the respondent's and the partner's self-reports. Comparisons of these two subjective reports may produce two different assessments of the "same" phenomena, showing response biases that may themselves serve as variables in a research study. At present, however, only one partner's self-reported answers to a questionnaire are often used as data and usually considered an accurate observation. In some studies where data are obtained from both spouses, researchers eliminate data from those couples where partners contradict each other. By including data from both intimate partners, more could be done to determine the type and extent of response bias that operate in subjective self-reports.

Lack of Behavioral Data. Research on intimates in conflict within the cognitive–exchange paradigm has also been criticized for seldom including "objectively observed" behaviorally coded data along with self-reports. The utility of different measures depends on the purposes of the assessment. When it is more useful to understand how the individual partner's perceptions guide his or her behavior than it is to understand the behavior itself, self-report measures may be the more appropriate measure to use. Advocates of the questionnaire approach claim that the data reflect the partner's own perceptions of certain types of behaviors during a conflict. The assumption that the partner's subjective evaluation constitutes an important determinant of behavior has received much support in the literature on conflict and marriage. Margolin (1990) suggests that the lack of agreement between "insiders" and "outsiders" does not mean that one or another observer provides more accurate or more useful information but means that they measure different types of information. It is thought that "outsiders" miss the more emotionally involved interpretation of partners' remarks that characterize spousal interaction.

Moreover, due to the nature of interaction typical in certain situations or types of relationships, it may be impossible to obtain data by any means but self-reports (e.g., awareness of feelings such as marital satisfaction, uniqueness of perspectives, attitudes toward partner, values differences, and sexual behavior). Thus, self-report measures are often necessary when subjective, personal, or socially sensitive data are needed.

There are times, however, when behavioral data may be needed, too. Take, for example, the following question: Do partners who report that they would use one conflict management strategy or another actually behave that way during conflict? Using Australians as respondents, Kabanoff (1987) found no significant correlations between observed behaviors and strategies of conflict resolution. If one tends to respond to dissatisfaction in a particular way on paper or indicates a preference for a particular conflict strategy, to what extent is he or she likely to actually behave in that manner? Research might be conducted to determine the conditions under which partners behave in a manner consistent with their preferred conflict management strategies.

Another problem comes when self-report measures are used as convenient substitutes for more reliable objective behavioral measures, unless great pains are taken to show that the self-reports correlate highly with behavioral measures. Otherwise, asking respondents to recall their own or their partner's behaviors in a specific situation on a pencil-and-paper test should not take the place of more demanding but more accurate methods involving videotaping interactions and training raters to accurately code them (see Chapter 2).

From the cognitive–exchange perspective, it is assumed that cognitions produce other cognitions *and behaviors*. It is believed that intimate behavior is based on cognition—namely, a perceived rewards–cost ratio that is derived from an internal CL and a CL-alt. Differences in perceived reward–cost ratios help explain why men "fall in love" more quickly than women, and why later women "fall out of love" sooner than men. Sources of conflict consist of a general concept of relationship dissatisfaction or specific sources like imbalance in resource exchange, inequity or unfairness, and inequality of power. One way or another, communication is believed to play an important role in relationship development. Educating intimates in conflict ranges from learning confrontation to avoidance techniques including cognitive restructuring, productive ambiguity, reorganization of one's priorities, and clarifying perspectives.

FIVE EPILOGUE

Empirical studies have meaning by their relationship to research traditions as well as by the statements they attempt to make. The researcher's task is to interpret and contribute to a way of perceiving reality by relating to paradigms and addressing theoretical questions as well as immediate practical ones. This book cuts across disciplines, relevant research paradigms, and theoretical concerns to explicate the work of others. To this end, the preceding chapters emphasize the dominant research paradigms as frameworks for organizing and better understanding many research studies and clarify their contributions to a complex, diffuse, multifaceted, and multidisciplinary literature that represents the study of conflict in intimate relationships.

In addition to interpreting findings within the context of a particular research perspective, an additional reason for tying specific studies to paradigms is to encourage scholars to work more within them. A number of studies on conflict between intimates were not included in this book because they did not relate clearly to one of the dominant paradigms. Relating one's research to an existing paradigm offers the following advantages.

1. *A paradigm has its own definition of conflict.* When research lacks awareness of the appropriate paradigm, there is inconsistency or vagueness in the definition of conflict. Systems–interactionists

define conflict as a stochastic process (see Chapter 2) involving interaction between persons who express opposing interests, views, or opinions. According to this approach a couple's conflict communication is categorized as positive or negative according to its effects on the intimate nature of the couple's relationship.

Rules–interventionists view conflict as a structured activity involving mediation in which a neutral third party assists divorcing partners in the process of resolving disputes. The structural approach to divorce mediation emphasizes the mediator's role as rule creator and enforcer to help partners establish lines of communication and produce successful mediation outcomes.

Cognitive–exchange researchers see conflict as cause and effect involving self–other perceptions and cognitive strategies that range from direct confrontation to avoidance. Since these cognitions are internal psychological constructs, partners have to report their internal states for others to "observe" them.

2. *A paradigm has its own theories and research methods.* Systems–interactionists advance information, cybernetics, and general systems theories and apply behaviorally based methods to record sources of conflict and to objectively code dyadic interaction usually from audio/videotapes.

Rules–interventionists advance mediation, rules and normative force, and intervention theories and apply behaviorally based methods to objectively code triadic interaction (partners and mediator) from tape-recorded mediation sessions.

Cognitive–exchange researchers advance social exchange, investment, social network, and social perception theories and apply cognition-based self-report questionnaires filled out by the partners involved.

3. *A paradigm has its own theoretical and methodological issues.* The following suggestions are only a few that are possible and certainly are not exhaustive. Systems–interactionists attempt to answer the question: How can a couple engage in problem solving without doing (more) harm to their intimate relationship? As they research this question, systems–interactionists could do comparative research to determine which negative conflict communication behav-

iors have the greatest impact or appear most negative? Different researchers have examined different conflict behaviors—for example, displeasing statement, expression of negative emotions (anger, fear, upset), an attempt to control/dominate, complain, blame, personal rejection/putdown, and other verbal abuses. Researchers could videotape dyadic interaction, manipulate one behavior at a time, and measure the impact of these changes on raters. Perhaps a comparative study would reveal that some negative conflict behaviors are rated as more harmful and destructive than others.

Regarding methodological issues, just because two or more raters agree on how to rate a particular behavior does not mean that they are in fact observing that behavior. For example, one partner may attempt to respond in a supportive manner, which is interpreted as such by his or her partner but is viewed otherwise by two raters. In this case, both raters may agree but are in error. Therefore, it would be useful to devise a means separate and different from the rating/coding process to establish what behavior actually occurs.

Rules–interventionists design research to answer the question: What role does the mediator play in helping divorcing couples restore communication and successfully resolve disputes? To this end, rules–interventionists need to conduct a great deal more empirical research. While there are a number of humanistic and deductive essays on the topic, there are only a few empirical studies on the role of the interventionist in divorce mediation. One reason for this may be that the rules–interventionist approach to the study of divorce mediation is "newer" as an empirical research paradigm than the others discussed in this book. While the role of the mediator has been of great interest since the inception of mediation, it is only recently that the rules–interventionist paradigm has emerged as a potentially dominant research approach. As it grows in acceptance, trends and insights may be gained.

At least two measures have been adapted to divorce mediation, but perhaps efforts could be directed toward creating a measure out of the process of divorce mediation itself. Donohue and his colleagues have developed a measure originally designed for coding plaintiff–defendant interaction negotiation, based on the Rogers and Farace relational control scheme. Slaikeu and his colleagues have based their scheme on one originally designed for coding interaction in marital problem solving. Although both adapted their measures to divorce mediation, there may be important variables that are not included in either measure. Moreover, the theoretical importance to divorce mediation of two key variables—relational control (competition–cooperation dichotomy) and affect (tone of voice)—may require the development of a single or combined instrument that measures both.

Research conducted within the cognitive–exchange perspective examines the role played by partners' cognitions (i.e., self–other perceptions and conflict management strategies) in relationship development or commitment. Questions of interest are among the following: What antecedent conditions influence one's choice of conflict management strategy? What alternative strategies are best for dealing with different sources of conflict?

As they pursue answers to these and other questions, cognitive–exchange researchers face a number of issues. One theoretical issue concerns a possible interrelationship among Rusbult's alternative responses to sources of conflict (the exit/voice/loyalty/neglect typology). As pointed out in Chapter 4, partners may progress through different types of response as dissatisfaction grows. For example, Healey and Bell (1990) argue that partners might prefer loyalty at first, hoping that things will get better soon. They may turn to "giving voice" when the situation does not improve, resort to partner neglect when that fails, and exit the relationship when all else fails. Longitudinal research could be designed to study responses to sources of conflict as a dynamic process over time.

Another theoretical issue involves the relationship between specific sources of conflict (e.g., inequity, imbalance in resource exchange, unequal power distribution) and a preference for certain conflict management strategies. For example, Roloff and Cloven (1990) point to a "chilling effect" in which partners low in power tend to prefer avoidance of conflict strategies. More research of this type needs to be done to tie particular strategies to specific sources of conflict.

Finally, future research should also give attention to conflict as a symptom of a problem and conflict as a cause of a problem. Both relationship dissatisfaction and preference for a conflict management strategy may be effects of deeper problems in an intimate relationship. For example, a couple may be both unhappy and express a preference for frequent confrontation because one of the partners is perceived as openly flirtatious and seductive around others. Meanwhile, conflict management strategies may cause unhappiness in couples. For example, a couple may be dissatisfied because one partner prefers extreme avoidance strategies and the other prefers overly aggressive confrontational strategies. Research is needed to determine whether conflict management as a cause and as an effect both equally affect relationship satisfaction and commitment.

In addition to the advancement of theory, there are several methodological issues for cognitive–exchange researchers to pursue. One way to investigate the role of subjective distortions in the self-reporting process is to include both the respondent's and the partner's self-reports. A comparison of these two subjective reports may produce two different assessments of the "same" phenomena, showing response biases that may themselves serve as variables in a research study. Normally researchers use only one partner's self-report and consider it an accurate observation. In addition, some researchers eliminate data from those couples whose partners disagree in their perceptions or subjective assessments of a phenomenon. By including data from both intimate partners, more can be done to determine the type and extent of response bias that operates in subjective self-reports.

There are also times when behavioral data are needed to determine whether partners engage in conflict behavior that is consistent with their reported preference for a particular conflict management strategy. Kabanoff (1987) questions the relationship between cognition and behavior. Research might be conducted to determine the conditions under which partners behave in a manner consistent with their preferred conflict management strategies.

Finally, there is a question whether the instruments, derived in the area of business management using employees as respondents, are appropriate as measures of conflict management strategies in intimate relationships. Research needs to be conducted to determine what significant differences exist between intimate and nonintimate relationships involving conflict and what instruments should be designed that are sensitive to these differences.

4. *A paradigm may tie the study of conflict into a useful concern of general interest that encourages others to also do research or support research on the topic.* Systems–interactionists have discovered that one way to generate interest in the topic of conflict communication behavior is to relate it to relationship or marital satisfaction. By distinguishing between satisfied and dissatisfied subjects, researchers are able to (a) observe dyadic patterns of conflict communication in both groups to determine if and how they differ, and (b) measure changes from pretest (assessment) to posttest (reassessment) when evaluating the effectiveness of behavioral and marital therapeutic methods.

Rules–interventionists tie their research to successful mediation outcomes. By distinguishing between mediation sessions that result in successful dispute resolution and subsequent compliance by partners from those that failed to end that way, researchers are able to identify triadic communication patterns involving mediator intervention that contribute to more successful mediation outcomes.

Cognitive–exchange researchers link their study of the topic of conflict to relationship development. By distinguishing stable from unstable relationships, researchers are able to identify cognitive variables in the form of social exchange and conflict management strategies that contribute to relationship growth (i.e., toward greater relationship satisfaction and commitment).

Alberts (1990) notes that "although it is unlikely that people are more contentious now than in decades past, certainly there has been increased focus by both scholars and popular writers on the causes and consequences of conflict" (p. 105). To the extent that the study of conflict is important in the development of intimate relationships, this book argues that a better understanding is achieved by relating theory and research to the appropriate research paradigm.

REFERENCES

Acitelli, L. K. (1988). When spouses talk to each other about their relationship. *Journal of Social and Personal Relationships, 5,* 185–199.

Alberts, J. K. (1990). The use of humor in managing couples' conflict interactions. In D. D. Cahn (Ed.), *Intimates in conflict: A communication perspective* (pp. 105–120). Hillsdale, NJ: Erlbaum.

Allen, M., & Donohue, W. (1987). The mediator as an arguer. In J. W. Wenzel (Ed.), *Argument and critical practices* (pp. 279–284). Annandale, VA: SCA.

Argyle, M., & Furnham, A. (1983). Sources of satisfaction and conflict in long term relationships. *Journal of Marriage and the Family, 45,* 481–493.

Aronson, D. (1974). Stimulus factors and listening strategies in auditory memory: A theoretical analysis. *Cognitive Psychology, 6,* 108–132.

Bach, G. R., & Wyden, P. (1968). *The intimate enemy.* New York: Avon.

Bahr, S. J. (1981). Mediation is the answer: Why couples are so positive about this route to divorce. *Family Advocate, 3,* 32–35.

Bahr, S. J., Chappell, C., & Marcos, A. C. (1987). An evaluation of a trial mediation program. *Mediation Quarterly, 18,* 37–52.

Baker-Miller, J. (1977). *Toward a new psychology of women.* Boston: Beacon.

Bales, R. F. (1950). *Interaction process analysis: A method for the study of small groups.* Cambridge, MA: Addison-Wesley.

Banks, S. P., Altendorf, D. M., Greene, J. O., & Cody, M. J. (1987). An examination of relationship disengagement: Perceptions, breakup strategies and outcomes. *Western Journal of Speech Communication, 51,* 19–41.

Barnett, L. R., & Nietzel, M. T. (1979). Relationship of instrumental and affectional behaviors and self-esteem to marital satisfaction in distressed and nondistressed couples. *Journal of Consulting and Clinical Psychology, 47*, 946–957.

Barsky, M. (1983). Emotional needs and dysfunctional communication as blocks to mediation. *Mediation Quarterly, 2*, 55–65.

Baucom, D. H., & Mehlman, S. K. (1984). Predicting marital status following behavioral marital therapy: A comparison of models of marital relationships. In K. Hahlweg & N. S. Jacobson (Eds.), *Marital interaction: Analysis and modification* (pp. 89–104). New York: Guilford .

Bautz, B. J., & Hill, R. M. (1989). Divorce mediation in New Hampshire: A voluntary concept. *Mediation Quarterly, 7*, 33–40.

Baxter, L. A., & Dindia, K. (1990). Marital partners' perceptions of marital maintenance strategies. *Journal of Social and Personal Relationships, 7*, 187–208.

Beck, E. A., & Beck, C. E. (1985). Improving communication in divorce mediation. *Journal of Divorce, 8*, 167–176.

Beisecker, T. (1970). Verbal persuasive strategies in mixed-motive interactions. *Quarterly Journal of Speech, 56*, 149–160.

Bell, E. C., & Blakeney, R. N. (1977). Personality correlates of conflict resolution modes. *Human Relations, 30*, 849–857.

Bernardin, H. J., & Alvarez, K. (1976). The managerial grid as a predictor of conflict resolution method and managerial effectiveness. *Administrative Science Quarterly, 21*, 84–92.

Berryman-Fink, C., & Brunner, C. (1987). The effects of sex of source and target on interpersonal conflict management styles. *Southern Speech Communication Journal, 53*, 38–48

Billings, A. (1979). Conflict resolution in distressed and nondistressed married couples. *Journal of Consulting and Clinical Psychology, 47*, 368–376.

Birchler, G. R., Weiss, R. L., & Vincent, J. P. (1975). Multimethod analysis of social reinforcement exchange between maritally distressed and nondistressed spouse and stranger dyads. *Journal of Personality and Social Psychology, 31*, 349–360.

Blake, R. R., & Mouton, J. S. (1964). *The managerial grid.* Houston, TX: Gulf.

Blau, P. M. (1964). *Exchange and power in social life.* New York: Wiley.

Bohannan, P. (1970). The six stations of divorce. In P. Bohannan (Ed.), *Divorce and after* (pp. 29–55). New York: Doubleday.

Booth, A., & Welch, S. (1978). Spousal consensus and its correlates: A reassessment. *Journal of Marriage and the Family, 40*, 23–32.

Braiker, H. B., & Kelley, H. H. (1979). Conflict in the development of close relationships. In R. L. Burgess & T. L. Huston (Eds.), *Social exchange in developing relationships* (pp. 135–168). New York: Academic Press.

Broderick, C., & Smith, J. (1979). The general systems approach to the family. In W. R. Burr, R. Hill, F. I. Nye, & I. L. Reiss (Eds.), *Contemporary theories about the family* (Vol. 1, pp. 112–129). New York: Free Press.

Burke, R. J. (1970). Methods of resolving superior-subordinate conflict: The constructive use of subordinate differences and disagreements. *Organizational Behavior and Human Performances, 5*, 393–411.

Burr, W. (1973). *Theory construction and the sociology of the family.* New York: Wiley.

Burrell, N. A., Donohue, W. A., & Allen, M. (1990). The impact of disputants' expectations on mediation: Testing an interventionist model. *Human Communication Research, 17*, 104–139.

Buss, D. M. (1989). Conflict between the sexes: Strategic interference and evocation of anger and upset. *Journal of Personality and Social Psychology, 56*, 735–747.

Buttny, R. (1990). Blame-account sequences in therapy: The negotiation of relational meanings. *Semiotica, 78*, 219–247.

Cahn, D. (1985). Communication competence in the resolution of intercultural conflict. *World Communication, 14*, 85–94.

Cahn, D. (1987). *Letting go: A practical theory of relationship disengagement and reengagement.* Albany, NY: State University of New York.

Cahn, D. (1990). Intimates in conflict: A research review. In D. D. Cahn (Ed.), *Intimates in conflict: A communication perspective* (pp. 1–22). Hillsdale, NJ: Erlbaum.

Canary, D. J., Cunningham, E. M., & Cody, M. J. (1988). Goal types, gender, and locus of control in managing interpersonal conflict. *Communication Research, 15*, 426–447.

Canary, D. J., & Spitzberg, B. H. (1987). Appropriateness and effectiveness perceptions of conflict strategies. *Human Communication Research, 14*, 93–118.

Canary, D. J., & Spitzberg, B. H. (1989). A model of the perceived competence of conflict strategies. *Human Communication Research, 15*, 630–649.

Canary, D. J., & Spitzberg, B. H. (1990). Attribution biases and associations between conflict strategies and competence outcomes. *Communication Monographs, 57*, 139–151.

Chafetz, J. (1980). Conflict resolution in marriage: Toward a theory of spousal strategies and marital dissolution rates. *Journal of Family Issues,* *1,* 397–421.

Chandler, D. B., & Chandler, S. M. (1987). Mediating the end of love. *Journal of Social Work & Human Sexuality, 5,* 123–136.

Christensen, A., & Heavey, C. L. (1990). Gender and social structure in the demand/withdraw pattern of marital conflict. *Journal of Personality and Social Psychology, 59,* 73–81.

Chusmir, L. H., & Mills, J. (1989). Gender differences in conflict resolution styles of managers: At work and at home. *Sex Roles, 20,* 149–163.

Cleek, M. G., & Pearson, T. A. (1985). Perceived causes of divorce: An analysis of interrelationships. *Journal of Marriage and the Family, 47,* 179–183.

Cloven, D. H., & Roloff, M. E. (1991). Sense-making activities and interpersonal conflict: Communicative cures for mulling the blues. *Western Journal of Speech Communication, 55,* 134–158.

Coogler, O. J. (1978). *Structured mediation in divorce settlement.* Lexington, MA: Lexington Books.

Coogler, O. J., Weber, R. E., & McKenry, P. C. (1979). Divorce mediation: A means of facilitating divorce and adjustment. *The Family Coordinator, 28,* 255–263.

Cooley, R. E., & Roach, D. A. (1984). A conceptual framework. In R. N. Bostrom (Ed.), *Competence in communication* (pp. 11–32). Beverly Hills, CA: Sage.

Coombs, C. H. (1987). The structure of conflict. *American Psychologist, 42,* 355–363.

Coombs, C. H., & Avrunin, G. S. (1988). *The structure of conflict.* Hillsdale, NJ: Erlbaum.

Cosier, R. A., & Ruble, T. L. (1981). Research on conflict-handling behavior: An experimental approach. *Academy of Management Journal, 24,* 816–831.

Crohan, S. E. (1992). Marital happiness and spousal consensus on beliefs about marital conflict: A longitudinal investigation. *Journal of Social and Personal Relationships, 9,* 89–102.

Crosby, J. F., Gage, B. A., & Raymond, M. C. (1983). The grief resolution process in divorce. *Journal of Divorce, 7,* 3–18.

Crowne, D. P., & Marlowe, D. (1960). A new scale of social desirability independent of psychopathology. *Journal of Consulting Psychology, 14,* 349–354.

Cupach, W. R. (1982, May). *Communication satisfaction and interpersonal solidarity as outcomes of conflict message strategy use.* Paper presented at the Annual Meeting of the International Communication Association, Boston, MA.

Cushman, D. P., & Cahn, D. (1985). *Communication in interpersonal relationships.* Albany, NY: State University of New York.

Cushman, D. P., & Whiting, G. (1972). An approach to communication theory: Toward consensus on rules. *Journal of Communication 22,* 217–238.

Deutsch, M. (1973). *The resolution of conflict: Constructive and destructive processes.* New Haven, CN: Yale University.

Donohue, W. A. (1981). Analyzing negotiation tactics: Development of a negotiation interact system. *Human Communication Research, 7,* 273–287.

Donohue, W. A., Allen, M., & Burrell, N. (1985). Communication strategies in mediation. *Mediation Quarterly, 10,* 75–89.

Donohue, W. A., Allen, M., & Burrell, N. (1988). Mediator communicative competence. *Communication Monographs, 55,* 104–119.

Donohue, W. A., Burrell, N., & Allen, M. (1989). Models of divorce mediation. *Conciliation Court Review, 54,* 409–420.

Donohue, W. A., & Weider-Hatfield, D. (1988). Communication strategies. In J. Folberg & A. Milne (Eds.), *Divorce mediation: Theory and practice* (pp. 297–315). New York: Guilford Press.

Druckman, D. (1977). Social–psychological approaches to the study of negotiation. In D. Druckman (Ed.), *Negotiations: Social psychological perspectives* (pp. 15–44). Beverly Hills, CA: Sage.

Duck, S. (1988). *Relating to others.* Chicago: Dorsey.

Emerson, R. M. (1976). Social exchange theory. In A. Inkles, J. Coleman, & N. Smelser (Eds.), *Annual review of sociology* (Vol. 2, pp. 335–362). Palo Alto, CA: Annual Reviews.

Emerson, R. M. (1981). Social exchange theory. In M. Rosenberg & R. Turner (Eds.), *Social psychology: Sociological perspectives* (pp. 30–65). New York: Basic Books.

Emery, R. E., & Wehr, M. M. (1987). Divorce mediation. *American Psychologist, 42,* 472–480.

Falloon, I. R. H., & Lillie, F. J. (1988). Behavioral family therapy: An overview. In I. R. H. Falloon (Ed.), *Handbook of behavioral family therapy* (pp. 3–26). New York: Guilford Press.

Fincham, F. D., & Bradbury, T. N. (1987a). Cognitive processes and conflict in close relationships: An attribution–efficacy model. *Journal of Personality and Social Psychology, 53,* 1106–1118.

Fincham, F. D., & Bradbury, T. N. (1987b). The assessment of marital quality: A reevaluation, *Journal of Marriage and the Family, 49*, 797–809.

Fincham, F. D., & Bradbury, T. N. (1991). Marital conflict: Towards a more complete integration of research and treatment. In J. Vincent (Ed.), *Advances in family intervention, assessment and theory* (Vol. 5, pp. 1–24). London: Jessica Kingsley.

Fincham, F. D., Bradbury, T. N., & Grych, J. H. (1990). Conflict in close relationships: The role of intrapersonal phenomena. In S. Graham & V. Folkes (Eds.), *Attribution theory: Applications to achievement, mental health, and interpersonal conflict* (pp. 161–184). Hillsdale, NJ: Erlbaum.

Fineberg, B. L., & Lowman, J. (1975). Affect and status dimensions of marital adjustment. *Journal of Marriage and the Family, 37*, 155–160.

Fisher, B. A. (1978). *Perspectives on human communication.* New York: Macmillan.

Fisher, R., & Ury, W. (1981). *Getting to yes.* Boston: Houghton Mifflin.

Fitzpatrick, M. A. (1988). *Between husbands & wives: Communication in marriage.* Beverly Hills, CA: Sage.

Fitzpatrick, M. A., & Winke, J. (1979). You always hurt the one you love: Strategies and tactics in interpersonal conflict. *Communication Quarterly, 27*, 3–11.

Floyd, F. J., & Markman, H. J. (1983). Observational biases in spouse observation: Toward a cognitive/behavioral model of marriage. *Journal of Consulting and Clinical Psychology, 51*, 450–457.

Foa, U. G., & Foa, E. B. (1974). *Societal structures of the mind.* Springfield, IL: Thomas.

Folberg, J., & Taylor, A. (1984). *Mediation.* San Francisco: Jossey-Bass.

Franzoi, S. L., Davis, M. H., & Young, R. D. (1985). The effects of private self-consciousness and perspective taking on satisfaction in close relationships. *Journal of Personality and Social Psychology, 48*, 1584–1594.

Gaelick, L., Bodenhausen, G. V., & Wyer, R. S. (1985). Emotional communication in close relationships. *Journal of Personality and Social Psychology, 49*, 1246–1265.

Genshaft, J. L. (1980). Perceptual and defensive style variables in marital discord. *Social Behavior and Personality, 8*, 81–84.

Girdner, L. K. (1985). Adjudication and mediation: A comparison of custody decision-making processes involving third parties. *Journal of Divorce, 8*, 33–47.

Goldner, V. (1985). Feminism and family therapy. *Family Process, 24*, 31–47.

Gordon, T. (1970). *Parent effectiveness training.* New York: Wyden.

Gottman, J. M. (1979). *Marital interaction: Experimental investigations.* New York: Academic Press.

Gottman, J. M. (1982a). Emotional responsiveness in marital conversations. *Journal of Communication, 16,* 108–119.

Gottman, J. M. (1982b). Temporal form: Toward a new language for describing relationships. *Journal of Marriage and the Family, 44,* 943–962.

Gottman, J. M. (1990). Finding the laws of close personal relationships. In I. E. Sigel & G. H. Brody (Eds.), *Methods of family research: Biography of research projects: Normal families* (Vol. 1, pp. 249–263). Hillsdale, NJ: Erlbaum.

Gottman, J. M. (1991). Predicting the longitudinal course of marriages. *Journal of Marital and Family Therapy, 17,* 3–7.

Gottman, J. M., & Levenson, R. W. (1986). Assessing the role of emotion in marriage. *Behavioral Assessment, 8,* 31–48.

Gottman, J. M., Markman, H., & Notarius, C. (1977). The topography of marital conflict: A sequential analysis of verbal and nonverbal behavior. *Journal of Marriage and the Family, 39,* 461–477.

Gottman, J. M., Notarius, C. Gonso, J., & Markman, H. (1976). *A couple's guide to communication.* Champaign, IL: Research.

Gottman, J., Notarius, C., Markman, H., Bank, S., Yoppi, B., & Rubin, M. E. (1976). Behavior exchange theory and marital decision making. *Journal of Personality and Social Psychology, 34,* 14–23.

Grebe, S. C. (1988). Structured mediation and its variants: What makes it unique. In J. Folberg & A. Milne (Eds.), *Divorce mediation: Theory and practice* (pp. 225–248). New York: Guilford Press.

Green, R. G., & Sporakowski, M. J. (1983). The dynamics of divorce: Marital quality, alternative attractions and external pressures. *Journal of Divorce, 7,* 77–88.

Hahn, L. O. (1987). Customized mediation for 'hard cases.' *Conciliation Courts Review, 25,* 29–32.

Hallock, S. (1988). An understanding of negotiation styles contributes to effective reality therapy for conflict resolutions with couples. *Journal of Reality Therapy, 8,* 7–12.

Hammock, G. S., Richardson, D. R., Pilkington, C. J., & Utley, M. (1990). Measurement of conflict in social relationships. *Personality and Individual Differences, 11,* 577–583.

Harre, H., & Secord, P. (1972). *The explanation of social behavior.* Totowa, NJ: Littlefield, Adams & Co.

Hatfield, E., Utne, M. K., & Traupmann, J. (1979). Equity theory and intimate relationships. In R. L. Burgers & T. L. Huston (Eds.), *Social exchange in developing relationships* (pp. 99–133). New York: Academic Press.

Hawes, L. C., & Smith, D. H. (1973). A critique of assumptions underlying the study of communication in conflict. *Quarterly Journal of Speech, 62*, 423–435.

Hawkins, J. L., Weisberg, C., & Ray, D. (1980). Spouse differences in communication style: Preference, perception, behavior. *Journal of Marriage and Family, 42*, 585–593.

Haynes, J. M. (1981). *Divorce mediation: A practical guide for therapists and counselors.* New York: Springer.

Healey, J. G., & Bell, R. A. (1990). Assessing alternate responses to conflicts in friendship. In D. D. Cahn (Ed.), *Intimates in conflict: A communication perspective* (pp. 25–48). Hillsdale, NJ: Erlbaum.

Heider, F. (1958). *The psychology of interpersonal relations.* New York: Wiley.

Hill, C., Rubin, Z., & Peplau, L. (1976). Breakups before marriage: The end of 103 affairs. *Journal of Social Issues, 32*, 147–168.

Hocker, J. L., & Wilmot, W. W. (1985). *Interpersonal conflict* (2nd ed.). Dubuque, IA: Wm C. Brown.

Homans, G. (1961). *Social behavior: Its elementary forms.* New York: Harcourt Brace Jovanovich.

Hoover, K. R. (1984). *The elements of social scientific thinking* (3rd ed.). New York: St. Martin's.

Hops, H., Wills, T. A., Patterson, G. R., & Weiss, R. L. (1972). The marital interaction coding system (MICS). Unpublished manuscript, University of Oregon.

Infante, D. A., & Rancer, A. S. (1982). A conceptualization and measure of argumentativeness. *Journal of Personality Assessment, 46*, 72–80.

Infante, D. A., Rancer, A. S., & Womack, D. F. (1990). *Building communication theory.* Prospect Heights, IL: Waveland.

Jacobs, S., Jackson, S., Hallmark, J., Hall, B., & Stearns, S. A. (1987). Ideal argument in the real world: Making do in mediation. In J. W. Wenzel (Ed.), *Argument and critical practices* (pp. 291–298). Annandale, VA: SCA.

Jacobson, N. S. (1977). Problem solving and contingency contracting in the treatment of marital discord. *Journal of Consulting and Clinical Psychology, 45*, 92–100.

Jacobson, N. S. (1978). Specific and nonspecific factors in the effectiveness of a behavioral approach to the treatment of marital discord. *Journal of Consulting and Clinical Psychology, 46*, 442–452.

Jacobson, N. S., & Margolin, G. (1979). *Marital therapy: Strategies based on social learning and behavior exchange principles.* New York: Brunner/ Mazel.

Jones, R., & Melcher, B. (1982). Personality and the preference for modes of conflict resolution. *Human Relations, 35,* 649–658.

Jones, T. S. (1988). Phase structures in agreement and no-agreement mediation. *Communication Research, 15,* 470–495.

Kabanoff, B. (1987). Predictive validity of the MODE conflict instrument. *Journal of Applied Psychology, 72,* 160–163.

Kahn, M. (1970). Non-verbal communication and marital satisfaction. *Family Process, 9,* 449–456.

Kahn, J., Coyne, J. C., & Margolin, G. (1985). Depression and marital disagreement: The social construction of despair. *Journal of Social and Personal Relationships, 2,* 447–461.

Kaslow, F. W. (1984). Divorce mediation and its emotional impact on the couple and their children. *American Journal of Family Therapy, 12,* 58–66.

Kelley, H. H. (1971). *Attribution in social interaction.* New York: General Learning.

Kelley, H. H. (1979). *Personal relationships: Their structures and processes.* Hillsdale, NJ: Erlbaum.

Kelley, H. H., Berscheid, E., Christensen, A., Harvey, J. H., Huston, T. L., Levinger, G., McClintock, E., Peplau, L. A., & Peterson, D. R. (1983). *Close relationships.* New York: Freeman.

Kelley, H. H., Cunningham, J. D., Grisham, J. A., Lefebvre, L. M., Sink, C. R., & Yablon, G. (1978). Sex differences in comments made during conflict within close heterosexual pairs. *Sex Roles, 4,* 473–492.

Kelley, H. H., & Thibaut, J. W. (1978). *Interpersonal relations: A theory of interdependence.* New York: Wiley-Interscience.

Kiely, L. S., & Crary, D. R. (1986). Effective mediation: A communication approach to consubstantiality. *Mediation Quarterly, 12,* 37–49.

Kilmann, R. H., & Thomas, K. W. (1977). Developing a forced-choice measure of conflict-handling behavior: The mode instrument. *Educational and Psychological Measurement, 37,* 309–325.

Kipnis, D. (1976). *The power-holders.* New York: Academic Press.

Kleinke, C. L. (1977). Assignment of responsibility for marital conflict to husbands and wives: Sex stereotypes or a double standard? *Psychological Reports, 41,* 219–222.

Knudson, R., Sommers, A., & Golding, S. (1980). Interpersonal perception in mode of resolution in marital conflict. *Journal of Personality and Social Psychology, 38,* 751–763.

Kochan, T., & Jick, T. (1978). The public sector mediation process: A theory and empirical examination. *Journal of Conflict Resolution, 22,* 209–219.

Kolevzon, M. S., & Gottlieb, S. J. (1983). The impact of divorce: A multivariate study. *Journal of Divorce, 7,* 89–98.

Koren, P., Carlton, K., & Shaw, D. (1980). Marital conflict: Relations among behaviors,outcomes, and distress. *Journal of Consulting and Clinical Psychology, 48,* 460–468.

Krain, M. (1977). Effects of love and liking in premarital dyads. *Sociological Focus, 10,* 249–262.

Kressel, K. (1987). Clinical implications of existing research on divorce mediation. *American Journal of Family Therapy, 15,* 69–74.

Kressel, K., Jaffee, N., Tuchman, B., Watson, C., & Deutsch, M. (1980). A typology of divorcing couples: Implications for mediation and the divorce process. *Family Process, 19,* 101–116.

Lawrence, P. R., & Lorsch, J. W. (1967). *Organization and environment.* Boston: Harvard University Graduate School of Business Administration.

Leary, T. (1957). *Interpersonal diagnosis of personality.* New York: Ronald.

Lerman, L. G. (1984). Mediation of wife abuse cases: The adverse impact of informal dispute resolution on women, *Harvard Women's Law Journal, 7,* 57–113.

Levenson, R. W., & Gottman, J. M. (1983). Marital interaction: Physiological linkage and affective exchange. *Journal of Personality and Social Psychology, 45,* 587–597.

Levenson, R. W., & Gottman, J. M. (1985). Physiological and affective predictors of change in relationship satisfaction. *Journal of Personality and Social Psychology, 49,* 85–94.

Levinger, G. (1979). A social exchange view on the dissolution of pair relationships. In R. L. Burgess & T. L. Huston (Eds.), *Social exchange in developing relationships* (pp. 169–193). New York: Academic Press.

Levinger, G., & Breedlove, J. (1966). Interpersonal attraction and agreement: A study of marriage partners. *Journal of Personality and Social Psychology, 3,* 367–372.

Levi-Straus, C. (1969). *The elementary structures of kinship.* Boston: Beacon.

Lewis, R. (1973). Social reaction and the formation of dyads: An interactionist approach to mate selection. *Sociometry, 36,* 409–418.

Liberman, R. P. (1972). *A guide to behavior analysis and therapy.* New York: Pergamon Press.

Lloyd, S. A. (1987). Conflict in premarital relationships: Differential perceptions of males and females. *Family Relations, 36,* 290–294.

Lloyd, S. A. (1990). A behavioral self-report technique for assessing conflict in close relationships. *Journal of Social and Personal Relationships, 7,* 265–272.

Lloyd, S. A., & Cate, R. M. (1985). The developmental course of conflict in dissolution of premarital relationships. *Journal of Social and Personal Relationships, 2,* 179–194.

Locke, H., & Wallace, K. (1959). Short marital adjustment and prediction tests: Their reliability and validity, *Marriage and Family Living, 21,* 251–525.

Long, N., & Forehand, R. (1990). Parental divorce research. In G. H. Brody & I. E. Sigel (Eds.), *Methods of family research: Biographies of research projects: Clinical populations* (Vol. 2, pp. 135–157). Hillsdale, NJ: Erlbaum.

Luckey, E. (1962). Perceptual congruence of self and family concepts as related to marital interaction. *Sociometry, 25,* 234–250.

MacKinnon, R., MacKinnon, C., & Franken, M. (1984). Family strengths in long-term marriages. *Lifestyles: A Journal of Changing Patterns, 7,* 115–126.

Margolin, G. (1987). The multiple forms of aggressiveness between marital partners: How do we identify them? *Journal of Marital and Marital Therapy, 13,* 77–84.

Margolin, G. (1990). Marital conflict. In G. H. Brody & I. E. Sigel (Eds.), *Methods of family research: Biographies of research projects: Clinical populations* (Vol. 2, pp. 191–225). Hillsdale, NJ: Erlbaum.

Margolin, G., Burman, B., & John, R. S. (1989). Home observations of married couples reenacting naturalistic conflicts. *Behavioral Assessment, 11,* 101–118.

Margolin, G., Fernandez, V., Gorin, L., & Ortiz, S. (1982, November). *The conflict inventory: A measurement of how couples handle marital tension.* Paper presented at the Annual Meeting of the Association for the Advancement of Behavior Therapy, Los Angeles, CA.

Margolin, G., Michelli, J., & Jacobson, N. (1988). Assessment of marital dysfunction. In A. S. Bellack & M. Hersen (Eds.), *Behavioral Assessment: A Practical Handbook* (pp. 441–489). New York: Pergamon Press.

Margolin, G., & Wampold, B. (1981). Sequential analysis of conflict and accord in distressed and nondistressed marital patterns. *Journal of Consulting and Clinical Psychology, 49,* 554–567.

Markowitz, J. R., & Engram, P. S. (1983). Mediation in labor disputes and divorces: A comparative analysis. *Mediation Quarterly, 2,* 67–78.

Marthaler, D. (1989). Successful mediation with abusive couples. *Mediation Quarterly, 23,* 295–315.

Mead, D. E., Vatcher, G. M., Wyne, B. A., & Roberts, S. L. (1990). The comprehensive areas of change questionnaire: Assessing marital couples' presenting complaints. *American Journal of Family Therapy, 18,* 65–79.

Mehrabian, A. (1972). *Nonverbal communication.* New York: Aldine-Atherton.

Menaghan, E. (1982). Measuring coping effectiveness: A panel analysis of marital problems and coping efforts. *Journal of Health and Social Behavior, 23,* 220–234.

Milardo, R. M. (1983). Social networks and pair relationships: A review of substantive and measurement issues. *Sociology and Social Research, 68,* 1–18.

Miller, S., Nunnally, E. W., & Wackman, D. B. (1975). *Alive and aware: Improving communication in relationships.* Minneapolis, MN: Interpersonal Communication Programs.

Mills, J., & Chusmir, L. H. (1988). Managerial conflict resolution styles: Work and home differences. *Journal of Social Behavior and Personality, 3,* 303–316.

Milne, A. L. (1986). Divorce mediation: A process of self-definition and self-determination. In N. S. Jacobson & A. S. Gurman (Eds.), *Clinical handbook of marital therapy* (pp. 197–216). New York: Guilford Press.

Moore, C. W. (1986). *The mediation process: Practical strategies for resolving conflict.* San Francisco: Jossey-Bass.

Murphy, K. J. (1987). *Effective listening.* New York: Bantam.

Navran, L. (1967) Communication and adjustment in marriage. *Family Process, 6,* 173–180.

Neal, A. G., & Groat, H. T. (1976). Consensus in the marital dyad: Couples' perceptions of contraception, communication, and family life. *Sociological Focus, 9,* 317–329.

Newton, D. A., & Burgoon, J. K. (1990). Nonverbal conflict behaviors: Functions, strategies, and tactics. In D. D. Cahn (Ed.), *Intimates in conflict: A communication perspective* (pp. 77–104). Hillsdale, NJ: Erlbaum.

Nichols, R., & Stevens, L. (1957). *Are you listening?* New York: McGraw-Hill.

Nye, F. I. (1979). Choice, exchange, and the family. In W. R. Burr, R. Hill, F. I. Nye, & I. L. Reiss (Eds.), *Contemporary theories about the family* (Vol. 2, pp. 1–41). New York: Free Press.

Olson, D. H., & Ryder, R. G. (1970) Inventory of marital conflicts (IMC): An experimental interaction procedure. *Journal of Marriage and the Family, 32*, 443–448.

Orvis, B. R., Kelley, H. H., & Butler, D. (1976). Attribution conflict in young couples. In J. H. Harvey, W. Ickes, & R. F. Kidd (Eds.), *New directions in attribution research* (Vol. 1, pp. 353–388). Hillsdale, NJ: Erlbaum.

Parks, M., Stan, C., & Eggert, L. (1983) Romantic involvement and social network involvement. *Social Psychology Quarterly, 46*, 116–131.

Patterson, G. R., Hops, H., & Weiss, R. L. (1975). Interpersonal skills training for couples in early stages of conflict. *Journal of Marriage and the Family, 37*, 295–303.

Pearson, J. (1981). Child custody: Why not let the parents decide. *The Judges' Journal, 20*, 4–12.

Pearson, J., & Thoennes, N. (1985). Divorce mediation: An overview of research results. *Columbia Journal of Law and Social Problems, 19*, 451–484.

Pearson, J., Thoennes, N., & Vanderkooi, L. (1982). The decision to mediate: Profiles of individuals who accept and reject the opportunity to mediate contested child custody and visitation issues. *Journal of Divorce, 6*, 17–35.

Petrossi, M. (1987). Separation anxiety in divorced parents and the mediation process. *Conciliation Courts Review, 25*, 63–64.

Pike, G. R., & Sillars, A. L. (1985). Reciprocity of marital communication. *Journal of Social and Personal Relationships, 2*, 303–324.

Pistole, C. (1989). Attachment in adult romantic relationships: Style of conflict resolution and relationship satisfaction. *Journal of Social and Personal Relationships, 6*, 505–510.

Potapchuk, W., & Carlson, C. (1987). Using conflict analysis to determine intervention techniques. *Mediation Quarterly, 16*, 31–43.

Prunty, A., Klopf, D. W., & Ishii, S. (1990). Japanese and American tendencies to argue. *Psychological Reports, 66*, 802.

Putnam, L. L., & Jones, T. S. (1982). The role of communication in bargaining. *Human Communication Research, 8*, 262–280.

Rahim, M. A. (1983). A measure of styles of handling interpersonal conflict. *Academy of Management Journal, 26*, 368–376.

Rahim, M. A., & Bonoma, T. V. (1979). Managing organizational conflict: A model for diagnosis and intervention. *Psychological Reports, 44*, 1323–1344.

Rands, M., Levinger, G., & Mellinger, G. D. (1981). Patterns of conflict resolution and marital satisfaction. *Journal of Family Issues, 2*, 297–321.

Rapoport, A. (1964). *Strategy and conscience.* New York: Harper & Row.

Raush, H., Barry, W., Hertel, R., & Swain, M. (1974). *Communication, conflict and marriage.* San Francisco: Jossey-Bass.

Raush, H. L., Greif, A. C., & Nugent, J. (1979). Communication in couples and families. In W. R. Burr, R. Hill, F. I. Nye & I. L. Reiss (Eds.), *Contemporary theories about the family* (Vol. 1, pp. 468–489). New York: Free Press.

Reiches, N. A., & Harral, H. B. (1974). Argument in negotiation: A theoretical and empirical approach. *Speech Monographs, 41,* 36–48.

Remer, R., & de Mesquita, P. (1990). Teaching and learning the skills of interpersonal confrontation. In D. D. Cahn (Ed.), *Intimates in conflict: A communication perspective* (pp. 225–252). Hillsdale, NJ: Erlbaum.

Renwick, P. A. (1977). Effects of sex differences on the perception and management of conflict: An exploratory study. *Organizational Behavior and Human Performance, 19,* 403–415.

Rettig, K. D., & Bubolz, M. M. (1983). Interpersonal resource exchanges as indicators of quality of marriage. *Journal of Marriage and the Family, 45,* 497–509.

Rice, D. G., & Rice, J. K. (1986). Separation and divorce therapy. In N. S. Jacobson & A. S. Gurman (Eds.), *Clinical handbook of marital therapy* (pp. 279–299). New York: Guilford Press.

Rogers, L. E., & Farace, R. V. (1975). Analysis of relational communication in dyads: New measurement procedures. *Human Communication Research, 1,* 222–239.

Rogers, L. E., Millar, F. E., & Bavelas, J. B. (1985). Methods for analyzing marital conflict discourse: Implications of a systems approach. *Family Process, 24,* 175–187.

Roloff, M. E., & Cloven, D. H. (1990). The chilling effect in interpersonal relationships: The reluctance to speak one's mind. In D. D. Cahn (Ed.), *Intimates in conflict: A communication perspective* (pp. 49–76). Hillsdale, NJ: Erlbaum.

Roloff, M. E., & Greenberg, B. S. (1979). Sex differences in choice of modes of conflict resolution in real-life and television. *Communication Quarterly, 27,* 3–12.

Rosenthal, D. B., & Hautaluoma, J. (1988). Effects of importance of issues, gender, and power of contenders on conflict management style. *Journal of Social Psychology, 128,* 699–701.

Rusbult, C. (1980). Commitment and satisfaction in romantic associations: A test of the investment model. *Journal of Experimental Social Psychology, 16,* 172–186.

Rusbult, C. (1983). A longitudinal test of the investment model: The development (and deterioration) of satisfaction and commitment in heterosexual involvements. *Journal of Personality and Social Psychology, 45*, 101–117.

Rusbult, C.E, Johnson, D. J., & Morrow, G. D. (1986a). Determinants and consequences of exit, voice, loyalty, and neglect: Responses to dissatisfaction in adult romantic involvements. *Human Relations, 39*, 45–63.

Rusbult, C.E, Johnson, D. J., & Morrow, G. D. (1986b). Impact of couple patterns of problem solving on distress and nondistress in dating relationships. *Journal of Personality and Social Psychology, 50*, 744–753.

Rusbult, C. E., & Zembrodt, I. M. (1983). Responses to dissatisfaction in romantic involvements: A multidimensional scaling analysis. *Journal of Experimental Social Psychology, 19*, 274–293.

Rusbult, C. E., Zembrodt, I. M., & Gunn, L. K. (1982). Exit, voice, loyalty, and neglect: Responses to dissatisfaction in romantic involvements. *Journal of Personality and Social Psychology, 43*, 1230–1242.

Ryder, R. G., & Goodrich, D. W. (1966). Married couples' responses to disagreement. *Family Process, 5*, 30–42.

Sabatelli, R. M., & Cecil-Pigo, E. F. (1985). Relational interdependence and commitment in marriage. *Journal of Marriage and the Family, 47*, 931–937

Saposnek, D. (1983). Strategies in child custody mediation: A family system approach. *Mediation Quarterly, 2*, 29–54.

Sawyer, J., & Guetzkow, H. (1965). Bargaining and negotiation in international relations. In H. Kelman (Ed.), *International behavior: A social psychological analysis* (pp. 466–520). New York: Holt, Rinehart & Winston.

Scanzoni, J. (1979a). A historical perspective on husband-wife bargaining power and marital dissolution. In G. Levinger & O. C. Moles (Eds.), *Divorce and separation* (pp. 20–36). New York: Basic Books.

Scanzoni, J. (1979b). Social exchange and behavioral interdependence. In R. L. Burgess & T. L. Huston (Eds.), *Social exchange in developing relationships* (pp. 61–98). New York: Academic Press.

Scanzoni, J., & Polonko, K. (1980). A conceptual approach to explicit marital negotiation. *Journal of Marriage and the Family, 42*, 31–43.

Schaap, C. (1982). *Communication and adjustment in marriage.* Lisse, Switzerland: Swets & Zeitlinger.

Shannon, C. E., & Weaver, W. (1949). *The mathematical theory of communication.* Urbana, IL: University of Illinois.

Shockley-Zalabak, P. S., & Morley, D. D. (1984). Sex differences in conflict style preferences. *Communication Research Reports, 1,* 28–32.

Sillars, A. L. (1980a). Attributions and communication in roommate conflicts. *Communication Monographs, 47,* 180–200.

Sillars, A. L. (1980b). The sequential and distributional structure of conflict interactions as a function of attributions concerning the locus of responsibility and stability of conflicts. In D. Nimmo (Ed.), *Communication yearbook 4* (pp. 217–235). New Brunswick, NJ: Transaction.

Sillars, A. L., Pike, G. R., Jones, T. S., & Murphy, M. A. (1984). Communication and understanding in marriage. *Human Communication Research, 10,* 317–350.

Sillars, A. L., Pike, G. R., Jones, T. S., & Redmon, K. (1985). Communication and conflict in marriage. In R. Bostrom (Ed.), *Communication yearbook 8* (pp. 414–422). Beverly Hills, CA: Sage.

Skinner, B. F. (1938). *The behavior of organisms.* New York: Appleton.

Slaikeu, K. A., Culler, R., Pearson, J., & Thoennes, N. (1985). Process and outcome in divorce mediation. *Mediation Quarterly, 10,* 55–74.

Slaikeu, K. A., Pearson, J., Luckett, J., & Myers, F. C. (1985). Mediation process analysis: A descriptive coding system. *Mediation Quarterly, 10,* 25–53.

Spanier, G. B. (1976). Measuring dyadic adjustment: New scales for assessing the quality of marriage and similar dyads, *Journal of Marriage and the Family, 38,* 15–28.

Spanier, G. B., & Thompson, L. (1983). Relief and distress after marital separation. *Journal of Divorce, 7,* 31–49.

Sprenkle, D. H., & Storm, C. L. (1983). Divorce therapy outcome research: A substantive and methodological review. *Journal of Marital and Family Therapy, 9,* 239–258.

Sternberg, R. J., & Dobson, D. M. (1987). Resolving interpersonal conflicts: An analysis of stylistic consistency. *Journal of Personality and Social Psychology, 52,* 794–812.

Sternberg, R. J., & Soriano, L. J. (1984). Styles of conflict resolution. *Journal of Personal and Social Psychology, 47,* 115–126.

Stets, J. E. (1990). Verbal and physical aggression in marriage. *Journal of Marriage and the Family, 52,* 501–514.

Storaasli, R. D., & Markman, H. J. (1990). Relationship problems in the early stages of marriage: A longitudinal investigation. *Journal of Family Psychology, 4,* 80–98.

Straus, M. (1979). Measuring intrafamily conflict and violence: The conflict tactics (CT) scales. *Journal of Marriage and the Family, 41,* 75–88.

Strodtbeck, F. L. (1951). Husband–wife interaction over revealed differences. *American Sociological Review, 16,* 468–473.

Stuart, R. B. (1980). *Helping couples change: A social learning approach to marital therapy.* New York: Guilford Press.

Stuart, R. B., & Jacobson, B. (1986/1987). Principles of divorce mediation: A social learning theory approach. *Mediation Quarterly, 14/15,* 71–85.

Taylor, A. (1981). Toward a comprehensive theory of mediation. *Conciliation Courts Review, 19,* 1–12.

Taylor, A. (1988). A general theory of divorce mediation. In J. Folberg & A. Milne (Eds.), *Divorce mediation: Theory and practice* (pp. 61–82). New York: Guilford Press.

Teachman, J. D., & Polonko, K. (1990). Negotiating divorce outcomes: Can we identify patterns in divorce settlements? *Journal of Marriage and the Family, 52,* 129–139.

Thibaut, J., & Kelley, H. (1959). *The social psychology of groups.* New York: Wiley.

Thoennes, N. A., & Pearson, J. (1985). Predicting outcomes in divorce mediation: The influence of people and process. *Social Issues, 41,* 115–126.

Thomas, K. W., & Kilmann, R. H. (1974). *Thomas-Kilmann conflict mode instrument.* Tuxedo, NY: Xicom.

Thompson, L., & Spanier, G. B. (1983). The end of marriage and acceptance of marital termination. *Journal of Marriage and the Family, 45,* 103–113.

Ting-Toomey, S. (1983a). An analysis of verbal communication patterns in high and low marital adjustment groups. *Human Communication Research, 9,* 306–319.

Ting-Toomey, S. (1983b). Coding conversation between intimates: A validation study of the intimate negotiation coding system (INCS). *Communication Quarterly, 31,* 68–77.

Ting-Toomey, S. (1984). Perceived decision-making power and marital adjustment. *Communication Research Reports, 1,* 15–20.

Utne, M. K., Hatfield, E., Traupmann, J., & Greenberger, D. (1984). Equity, marital satisfaction, and stability. *Journal of Social and Personal Relationships, 1,* 323–332.

Vaughan, D. (1979). Uncoupling. *Alternative Lifestyles, 2,* 415–442.

Veltkamp, L. J., & Miller, T. W. (1988). Effects of family mediation on disputed child custody in divorce. *International Journal of Family Psychiatry, 9,* 417–430.

Vincent, J. P., Weiss, R. L., & Birchler, G. R. (1975). A behavioral analysis of problem solving in distressed and nondistressed married and stranger dyads. *Behavior Therapy, 6,* 475–487.

von Bertalanffy, L. (1968). *General system theory.* New York: Braziller.

von Wright, G. (1971). *Explanation and understanding.* Ithaca, NY: Cornell.

Wallerstein, J. S. (1986/1987). Psychodynamic perspectives on family mediation. *Mediation Quarterly 14/15,* 7–21.

Walster (Hatfield), E., Walster, G. W., & Berscheid, E. (1978). *Equity: Theory and research.* New York: Allyn and Bacon.

Watzlawick, P., Beavin, J., & Jackson, D. (1967). *Pragmatics of human communication: A study of interactional patterns, pathologies, and paradoxes.* New York: W. W. Norton.

Weiss, R. S. (1976). The emotional impact of marital separation. *Journal of Social Issues, 32,* 135–145.

Weiss, R., Hops, H., & Patterson, G. R. (1973). A framework for conceptualizing marital conflict: A technology for altering it, some data for evaluating it. In L. A. Hamerlynch, I. C. Handy, & E. J. Mash (Eds.), *Behavior change: Methodology, concepts and practice* (pp. 309–342). Champaign, IL: Research.

Weiss, R. L., & Perry, B. A. (1983). Assessment of conflict and accord: A second look. In A. Ciminero (Ed.), *Handbook of behavioral assessment* (Vol. 2, pp. 561–600). New York: Wiley.

Weiss, R. L., & Summers, K. J. (1983). Marital interaction coding system III. In E. E. Filsinger (Ed.), *Marriage and family assessment* (pp. 85–115). Beverly Hills, CA: Sage.

Werner, B. L. (1990). *I want the kids! Parents' conversational strategies during child custody mediation.* Paper presented at the annual meeting of the Speech Communication Association, Chicago, IL.

White, B. B. (1989). Gender differences in marital communication patterns. *Family Process, 28,* 89–106.

Wiener, N. (1948). *Cybernetics: Or control and communication in the animal and the machine.* Cambridge, MA: MIT.

Wills, T. A., Weiss, R. L., & Patterson, G. R. (1974). A behavioral analysis of the determinants of marital satisfaction. *Journal of Consulting and Clinical Psychology, 42,* 802–811.

Zammuto, R. F., London, M., & Rowland, K. W. (1979). Effects of sex on commitment and conflict resolution. *Journal of Applied Psychology, 64,* 227–231.

Zietlow, P. H., & Sillars, A. L. (1988). Life stage differences in communication during marital conflicts. *Journal of Social and Personal Relationships, 5,* 223–245.

AUTHOR INDEX

Acitelli, L. K., 98, 125
Alberts, J. K., 25, 31, 113, 123, 125
Allen, M., 5, 40, 48–49, 51–52, 125, 127, 129
Altendorf, D. M., 101, 125
Alvarez, K., 95, 126
Argyle, M., 47, 125
Aronson, D., 112, 125
Avrunin, G. S., 3, 128

Bach, G. R., 125
Bahr, S. J., 46–47, 125
Baker-Miller, J., 29, 125
Bales, R. F., 20, 125
Bank, S., 131
Banks, S., 101, 125
Barnett, L. R., 28, 125
Barry, W., 20, 138
Barsky, M., 50, 126
Baucom, D. H., 39, 126
Bautz, B. J., 46, 126
Bavelas, J. B., 14, 138
Baxter, L. A., 101, 126
Beavin, J., 5, 142
Beck, C. E., 50, 126
Beck, E. A., 50, 126
Beisecker, T., 50, 66, 126
Bell, E. C., 9, 106, 126
Bell, R. A., 92, 121, 132
Bernardin, H. J., 95, 126
Berryman-Fink, C., 96, 104–105, 126
Berscheid, E., 85, 133, 142
Billings, A., 20, 29, 87, 126
Birchler, G. R., 16, 21, 28, 101, 141
Blake, R. R., 94–95, 126
Blakeney, R. N., 9, 106, 126
Blau, P. M., 6, 73, 126
Bodenhausen, G. V., 29, 126, 130
Bohannan, P., 59, 126

Bonoma, T. V., 96, 137
Booth, A., 100, 126
Bradbury, T. N., 81–82, 108, 113, 129–130
Braiker, H. B., 2, 79, 113, 127
Breedlove, J., 100, 134
Broderick, C., 13, 127
Brunner, C., 96, 104–105, 126
Bubolz, M. M., 83, 138
Burgoon, J. K., 113, 136
Burke, R. J., 95, 127
Burman, B., 3, 135
Burr, W., 78, 127
Burrell, N., 5, 46, 49, 52, 129
Buss, D. M., 85, 127
Butler, D., 113, 137
Buttny, R., 35, 127

Cahn, D., 2, 47, 78, 89, 106, 110, 112, 127, 129
Canary, D. J., 81, 93–94, 98, 114, 127
Carlson, C., 68, 137
Carlton, K., 22, 134
Cate, R. M., 24, 135
Cecil-Pigo, E. F., 87, 98, 139
Chafetz, J., 89, 127
Chandler, D. B., 40, 128
Chandler, S. M., 40, 128
Chappell, C., 46, 125
Christensen, A., 31, 128, 133
Chusmir, L. H., 96, 104, 106–107, 128, 136
Cleek, M. G., 52, 128
Cloven, D. H., 99, 101, 103, 121, 128, 138
Cody, M. J., 93, 101, 125, 127
Coogler, O. J., 48, 51, 68–69, 128
Cooley, R. E., 52, 128
Coombs, C. H., 3, 128
Cosier, R. A., 96, 128
Coyne, J. C., 93, 133

Crary, D. R., 50, 68, 133
Crohan, S. E., 99, 128
Crosby, J. F., 60, 128
Crowne, D. P., 96, 128
Culler, R., 56–57, 63, 69, 140
Cunningham, E. M., 93, 127
Cunningham, J. D., 133
Cupach, W. R., 93, 128
Cushman, D. P., 47, 89, 129

Davis, M. H., 24, 130
de Mesquita, P., 111, 138
Deutsch, M., 49, 51–52, 54, 66, 129, 134
Dindia, K., 101, 126
Dobson, D. M., 105, 140
Donohue, W. A., 5, 40, 48–49, 51–52, 56–59,
    63, 69–71, 120, 125, 127, 129
Druckman, D., 66, 129
Duck, S., 23, 129

Eggert, L., 78, 137
Emerson, R. M., 6, 73, 129
Emery, R. E., 46, 129
Engram, P. S., 53, 135

Falloon, I. R., 34, 129
Farace, R. V., 56, 121, 138
Fernandez, V., 93, 114, 135
Fincham, F. D., 81–82, 108, 113, 129–130
Fineberg, B. L., 20, 39, 130
Fisher, B. A., 12, 130
Fisher, R., 69, 130
Fitzpatrick, M. A., 1, 26, 31, 90, 99, 102, 104,
    130
Floyd, F. J., 39, 130
Foa, E. B., 83, 130
Foa, U. G., 83, 130
Folberg, J., 67, 130
Forehand, R., 51, 135
Franken, M., 104, 135
Franzoi, S. L., 24, 130
Furnham, A., 47, 125

Gaelick, L., 29, 99, 130
Gage, B. A., 60, 128
Genshaft, J. L., 98, 130
Girdner, L. K., 44–45, 68, 130
Golding, S., 98, 133
Goldner, V., 105, 130
Gonso, J., 35, 81, 131
Goodrich, D. W., 25, 100, 139
Gordon, T., 69, 130
Gorin, L., 93, 114, 135
Gottlieb, S. J., 50, 134
Gottman, J. M., 11, 13, 16, 21–22, 25–26,
    28–31, 34–35, 38, 81, 131, 134
Grebe, S. C., 41, 49, 68, 131

Green, R. G., 78, 131
Greenberg, B. S., 104–105, 138
Greenberger, D., 85–86, 141
Greene, J. O., 101, 125
Greif, A. C., 13, 138
Grisham, J. A., 133
Groat, H. T., 100, 136
Grych, J. H., 81, 130
Guetzkow, H., 41, 139
Gunn, L. K., 88, 139

Hahn, L. O., 68, 131
Hall, B., 44, 132
Hallmark, J., 44, 132
Hallock, S., 96, 131
Hammock, G. S., 96, 131
Harral, H. B., 66, 138
Harre, H., 47, 131
Harvey, J. H., 133
Hatfield, E., 85, 132, 141–142
Hautaluoma, J., 96, 104, 138
Hawes, L. C., 23, 132
Hawkins, J. L., 29, 87, 132
Haynes, J. M., 45, 53, 132
Healey, J. G., 92, 121, 132
Heavey, C. L., 31, 128
Heider, F., 6, 81, 113
Hertel, R., 20, 138
Hill, C., 77, 83, 132
Hill, R. M., 46, 126
Hocker, J. L., 103, 132
Homans, G., 6, 73–74, 132
Hoover, K. R., 4, 132
Hops, H., 16, 20–21, 35, 132, 137, 142
Huston, T. L., 133

Infante, D. A., 4, 106, 132
Ishii, S., 106, 137

Jackson, D., 5, 142
Jackson, S., 44, 132
Jacobs, S., 44, 132
Jacobson, B., 52–52, 141
Jacobson, N. S., 34–36, 38, 108, 132–133,
    135
Jaffee, N., 52, 134
Jick, T., 62, 134
John, R. S., 3, 135
Johnson, D. J., 77, 89, 103, 139
Jones, R., 106, 133
Jones, T. S., 25, 41, 50, 55, 56–57, 64–67, 100,
    133, 137, 140

Kabanoff, B., 116, 122, 133
Kahn, J., 93, 133
Kahn, M., 81, 133
Kaslow, F. W., 45, 133

Kelley, H. H., 2, 6, 73–74, 79, 81, 105, 113, 127, 133, 137, 141
Kiely, L. S., 50, 68, 133
Kilmann, R. H., 95–96, 104, 133, 141
Kipnis, D., 90, 133
Kleinke, C. L., 105, 133
Klopf, D. W., 106, 137
Knudson, R., 98, 133
Kochan, T., 62, 134
Kolevzon, M. S., 50, 134
Koren, P., 22, 24, 28, 134
Krain, M., 78, 134
Kressel, K., 46, 52, 61–62, 66, 134

Lawrence, P. R., 95, 134
Leary, T., 20, 134
Lefebvre, L. M., 133
Lerman, L. G., 43, 61, 134
Levenson, R. W., 28, 30, 38, 131, 134
Levinger, G., 1, 75–78, 100, 111, 133–134, 137
Levi-Straus, C., 73, 134
Lewis, R., 78, 134
Liberman, R. P., 33, 134
Lillie, F. J., 34, 129
Lloyd, S. A., 24, 80, 134–135
Locke, H., 38, 135
London, M., 95, 104, 142
Long, N., 51, 135
Lorsch, J. W., 95, 134
Lowman, J., 20, 39, 130
Luckett, J., 57, 140
Luckey, E., 100, 135

MacKinnon, C., 104, 135
MacKinnon, R., 104, 135
Marcos, A. C., 46, 125
Margolin, G., 3, 21, 28–30, 35, 38–39, 93, 105, 108, 113–114, 116, 133, 135
Markman, H., 18, 28, 35, 39, 130–131, 140
Markowitz, J. R., 53, 135
Marlowe, D., 96, 128
Marthaler, D., 69, 135
McClintock, E., 133
McKenry, P. C., 51, 128
Mead, D. E., 17, 136
Mehlman, S. K., 39, 126
Mehrabian, A., 22, 29, 136
Melcher, B., 106, 133
Mellinger, G. D., 1, 137
Menaghan, E., 99–100, 104, 136
Michelli, J., 38, 135
Milardo, R. M., 78, 136
Millar, F. E., 14, 138
Miller, S., 112, 136
Miller, T. W., 51, 55, 61–62, 141
Mills, J., 96, 104, 106–107, 128, 136

Milne, A. L., 41, 54, 136
Moore, C. W., 67, 136
Morley, D. D., 96, 104–105, 140
Morrow, G. D., 77, 89, 103, 139
Mouton, J. S., 94–95, 126
Murphy, K. J., 112, 136
Murphy, M. A., 100, 140
Myers, F. C., 57, 140

Navran, L., 97, 136
Neal, A. G., 100, 136
Newton, D. A., 113, 136
Nichols, R., 112, 136
Nietzel, M. T., 28, 125
Notarius, C., 28, 35, 81, 131
Nugent, J., 13, 138
Nunnally, E. W., 112, 136
Nye, F. I., 75, 84, 136

Olson, D., 16, 136
Ortiz, S., 93, 114, 135
Orvis, B. R., 113, 137

Parks, M., 78, 137
Patterson, G. R., 15–16, 21, 132, 137, 142
Pearson, J., 46, 56–58, 60–64, 67, 137, 141
Pearson, T. A., 52, 128, 140
Peplau, L., 77, 132–133
Perry, B. A., 27, 142
Peterson, D. R., 133
Petrossi, M., 68, 137
Pike, G. R., 25–26, 30–31, 99–100, 137, 140
Pilkington, C. J., 96, 131
Pistole, C., 96, 103, 137
Polonko, K., 41, 61, 139, 141
Potapchuk, W., 68, 137
Prunty, A., 106, 137
Putnam, L. L., 41, 66, 137

Rahim, M. A., 95–97, 137
Rancer, A. S., 4, 106, 132
Rands, M., 1, 90, 99, 137
Rapoport, A., 69, 137
Raush, H. L., 13, 16, 20, 29, 138
Ray, D., 29, 132
Raymond, M. C., 60, 128
Redmon, K., 25, 140
Reiches, N. A., 66, 138
Remer, R., 111, 138
Renwick, P. A., 95, 104, 138
Rettig, K. D., 83, 138
Rice, D. G., 53, 138
Rice, J. K., 53, 138
Richardson, D. R., 96, 131
Roach, D. A., 52, 128
Roberts, S. L., 17, 136
Rogers, L. E., 14, 56, 121, 138

Roloff, M. E., 99, 101, 103–105, 121, 128, 138
Rosenthal, D. B., 96, 104, 138
Rowland, K. W., 95, 104, 142
Rubin, M. E., 131
Rubin, Z., 77, 132
Ruble, T. L., 96, 128
Rusbult, C., 74–77, 88–39, 91–92, 101, 103, 105, 110, 113, 121, 138–139
Ryder, R. G., 16, 25, 100, 136, 139

Sabatelli, R. M., 87, 98, 139
Saposnek, D., 67, 139
Sawyer, J., 41, 139
Scanzoni, J., 61, 75, 84, 98, 111, 139
Schaap, C., 22, 139
Secord, P., 47, 131
Shannon, C. E., 12, 139
Shaw, D., 22, 134
Shockley-Zalabak, P. S., 96, 104–105, 140
Sillars, A. L., 18, 23, 25–26, 30–31, 81, 93, 99–100, 113, 137, 140, 142
Sink, C. R., 133
Skinner, B. F., 10, 140
Slaikeu, K. A., 56–59, 63–64, 69, 121, 140
Smith, D. H., 23, 132
Smith, J., 13, 127
Sommers, A., 98, 133
Soriano, L. J., 104–106, 140
Spanier, G. B., 39, 41, 140, 141
Spitzberg, B. H., 81, 93–94, 98, 114, 127
Sporakowski, M. J., 78, 131
Sprenkle, D. H., 47, 140
Stan, C., 78, 137
Stearns, S. A., 44, 132
Sternberg, R. J., 104–106, 140
Stets, J. E., 3, 140
Stevens, L., 112, 136
Storaasli, R. D., 18, 140
Storm, C. L., 47, 140
Straus, M. A., 3, 93, 140
Strodtbeck, F. L., 16, 25, 101, 141
Stuart, R. B., 35, 52–53, 141
Summers, K. J., 28, 142
Swain, M., 20, 138

Taylor, A., 43, 66–67, 130, 141
Teachman, J. D., 41, 141
Thibaut, J. W., 73–74, 133, 141
Thoennes, N., 56, 60, 62, 67, 137, 140–141
Thomas, K. W., 95–96, 104, 133, 141
Thompson, L., 41, 140–141

Ting-Toomey, S., 1, 23, 28, 87, 98, 141
Traupmann, J., 85–86, 132, 141
Tuchman, B., 52, 134

Ury, W., 69, 130
Utley, M., 96, 131
Utne, M. K., 85–86, 98, 132, 141

Vanderkooi, L., 60, 137
Vatcher, G. M., 17, 136
Vaughan, D., 59, 141
Veltkamp, L. J., 51, 55, 61–62, 141
Vincent, J. P., 16, 21, 28, 126, 141
von Bertalanffy, L., 13, 142
von Wright, G., 48, 142

Wackman, D. B., 112, 136
Wallace, K., 39, 135
Wallerstein, J. S., 61, 142
Walster, E., 85–86, 142
Walster, G. W., 85, 142
Wampold, B., 21, 28–30, 135
Watson, C., 52, 134
Watzlawick, P., 5, 14, 142
Weaver, W., 12, 139
Weber, R. E., 51, 128
Wehr, M. M., 46, 129
Weider-Hatfield, D., 63, 129
Weisberg, C., 29, 132
Weiss, R. L., 15–16, 21, 27–28, 50, 107, 126, 132, 137, 141–142
Welch, S., 100, 126
Werner, B. L., 45, 62, 142
White, B. B., 29, 142
Whiting, G., 47, 129
Wiener, N., 11, 142
Wills, T. A., 15–16, 29, 132, 142
Wilmot, W. W., 103, 132
Winke, J., 1, 90, 99, 102, 104, 130
Womack, D. F., 4, 132
Wyden, P., 125
Wyer, R. S., 29, 130
Wyne, B. A., 17, 136

Yablon, G., 133
Yoppi, B., 131
Young, R. D., 24, 130

Zammuto, R. F., 95, 104, 142
Zembrodt, I. M., 88, 91, 139
Zietlow, P. H., 18, 142

SUBJECT INDEX

Abstract variables, 113
Adjudication, litigation, 45–46, 61
Affection, sexual relations, 17, 20, 22, 28, 39, 81, 84–85
Assessment of training, of therapy, 26, 33
Attribution process, 81
Avoidance strategies (unexpressed conflict), *see* Conflict management strategies

Behavior–cognition controversy, 114–117
Behavioral
  contracts, 33
  dyadic conflict observation systems, measures, 19–26
  modification, behavioral therapy, 33–34
  rehearsal, 34

Causality/cause–effect analysis, 47
Chilling effect, 121
Clarification of perceptions, 112
Coercive/controlling behaviors, 28–29
Cognitive
  restructuring, 108–109
  self-reports
    measures, 26–27, 38–39, 89–97
    uses and limitations of, 114–116, 122
Color matching test, 100–101
Commitment, 102–103
Communication
  competence, 52
  favorable attitudes toward, 61–62
  quality, 97–100
  rules, 47–49, 51, 70–71
  skills, 34–36
Comparison levels
  alternatives (CL-alt), 74–76
  neutral point (CL), 74–76
Competition, 49–50, 57, 65, 67
Conflict
  defined, 2, 9, 40, 72, 118–119
  dimensions, 20, 90, 95–96, 102

management strategies
  accommodating, smoothing, 94–97, 109–111
  avoiding, 23–26, 30–32, 72, 94–97, 99–101, 121–122
  collaborating, 94–97
  competing, forcing, aggression, 90, 94–97
  compromising, 94–97
resolution, 23–25, 50–51, 89, 107, 116
responses to conflict
  exit–voice–loyalty–neglect typology, 91–92, 101–102, 113–114, 121
sources of
  behavioral, 15–19
  mediated, 54–55
  cognitive, 83–89
stages of, 3–4
tactics, 3, 90, 93
typologies, 89–97
Conflicting (unhappy/dissolving) relation-ships, 3
Confrontation, 23–25, 97–99, 111
Context, *see* Culture; Life cycle; Relationship
Control over resources, 54; *see also* Re-sources of exchange
Cooperation, 49–50, 57, 65, 67
Coping strategies
  optimistic comparison, 104
  productive ambiguity, 110
  reorganizing priorities, 110
  resignation, 104
  selective ignoring, 194
Couple's history, 62
Culture, 106
Cybernetics theory, 11–13, 37

Disagreement
  daily observation records, 80
  specific disagreements, 2–3
Divorce, stations of, 59–60

Efficacy expectations, 81
Emotion, *see* Negative affect
Equity theory, 85–87, 117
Escalation, negative reciprocity, 29–30, 32–33

Family strengths, 103–104
Friendship, 6, 18, 40, 45, 47, 78–79, 96, 98

General systems theory, 13–15, 37

Hidden agendas, 36
Holism, 14, 32–33, 37
Homeostasis, 13, 33, 37
Human subjects' rights, 38

Information theory, 11–13, 37
Integrative/disintegrative communication
    patterns, 23, 25, 28
Intention (goals, purpose, reason), 48
Interdependence, *see* General systems the-
    ory
Intervention, 49
Intimacy, defined, 2
Investment theory, 76–77, 113
Issue salience, problem severity, 104

Language, 36
Life cycle, 18–19
Listening skills, 35, 69–70, 111–112
Love, 79, 83–84

Male–female/gender differences, 77, 80,
    104–105
Management of differences exercise, 95–96
Marital therapy, *see* Therapy
Mediation
    assumptions, 43–44
    defined, 40
    favorable attitudes, *see* Communication
    mediator's role, 49–52, 63–64, 68–70
    outcomes, benefits, agreements, 46–47
    phases, stages, 64, 66
    rules, *see* Communication rules
    structured, 35, 48–49, 57, 63, 67, 69
    triadic conflict interaction measures, 55–59
Metacommunication, 35–36
Microanalysis, 35
Modeling, 34

Negative affect, 27–28, 79–80
Negotiation, bargaining, 3, 40, 49, 51, 56,
    71, 111
Neutrality, impartiality, 49
Nonmutuality of the divorce decision, 60
Nonverbal behavior, 22, 26, 35
Normative force, *see* Rules theory

Paradigm
    case, 4
    defined, 4
    dominant research paradigms, 5–7
Perceptual processes, 80–82
Personality variables, 105–106
Power, 20, 22, 28–30, 61, 87, 103, 117
Problem solving discussion, 3

Reframing, 35, 57, 63, 67, 69
Relationship
    development, 113, 123; *see also* Commit-
        ment; Relationship satisfaction
    nature of, 54
    satisfaction/dissatisfaction, 1, 26–27, 87–
        89, 123
      measures, 38–39
    talk, 98
Resources of exchange, 83–84
Response bias, 115
Responsiveness, 22–23
Revealed difference technique, 16
Reward–cost ratio, 73–76, 80, 91–92, 113
Rigidity, 30
Role playing technique, 34
Rules governing relationship, social con-
    text, *see* Communication rules
Rule setting/enforcement, 51
Rules theory, 47–49

Self-assertion/disclosure, 58, 64, 77, 80,
    112
Sexual interests, 84–85; *see also* Affection
Social concerns, 50–51
Social exchange theory, 73–76
Social desirability, 95–96; *see also* Response
    bias
Social influence, 47–48, 78–79
Social learning theory, 10–11, 36
Spousal consensus, 100
Stimulus–response (reinforcement), 10
Stochastic process, 12, 47
Stone walling, 24

Theory, defined, 4
Therapy, 32–36, 52–53, 65–70, 107–112
Trust, 66–68

Uncertainty, 14, 30, 51

Videotaped interaction
    affect scanning procedure, 22
    disadvantages, 38
    split screen technique, 23

Zone of reasonableness, 41, 50